A Compendium of Canadian Folk Artists

A Compendium of Canadian
FOLK ARTISTS

Terry Kobayashi and Michael Bird

The Boston Mills Press

CANADIAN CATALOGUING IN PUBLICATION DATA

Kobayashi, Terry, 1939-
  A compendium of Canadian folk artists

Bibliography: p.
ISBN 0-919783-32-5

1. Folk art – Canada. 2. Primitivism in art –
Canada. I. Bird, Michael S., 1941-   II. Title.

NK841.K62 1985   709'.71   C85-098940-X

In their research for this book, the authors have endeavoured to compile a major volume of artists as presently known from articles, exhibitions and interviews. It is hoped that additional names can be published in future supplements as occasion permits. Any pertinent information which could be forwarded to the publisher would be greatly appreciated.

Published by The Boston Mills Press,
98 Main Street, Erin, Ontario N0B 1T0.
1-519-833-2407

The Boston Mills Press gratefully acknowledges the assistance of the Canada Council, the Ontario Arts Council, and the office of the Secretary of State.

The front cover is after a painting (oil on canvas, 1984) by Joe Norris entitled At Home on a Quiet Afternoon (photo by John Houston).

Typeset in Cartier by The Coach House Press (Toronto). Printed by the Porcupine's Quill, Inc. (Erin).

ISBN 0-919783-32-5

In memory of Dr. J. Russell Harper (1914-1983), scholar and friend.

Mr Murphy in Nfld?

Canadian Folk Art:
Contours of a Hazy Landscape

In the wake of many varying, if not conflicting discussions of folk art, the journey toward definition invariably takes us into highly unfamiliar terrain. This landscape, not always chartable in its remoter reaches, does nevertheless present certain features whose contours invite brief observations and demarcation.

Within what might otherwise seem to be an anarchic offering of definitions, significant patterns do emerge as central to the ongoing discussion. In particular, there is a two-track perspective, sometimes described as the distinction between a European and an American point of view.[1] The former tends to view folk art as a collective phenomenon, the latter as individual expression. On the one hand, folk art is defined as the collective manifestation of an ethnically-based decorative tradition. On the other hand, folk art comes to be seen rather as the product of the individual mind, the artistic outpouring of an untrained painter, sculptor or other practitioner. In both cases, the very idea of folk art is understood as a relative expression, in that it derives meaning in relationship to a reference point. In the former instance, the reference point is the traditional decorative motif; in the latter case, the reference point is formal art.[2]

In the defining process, much has been said about 'naive' or 'primitive' elements in art. Such words present numerous problems and require some elucidation, particularly as they pertain to the twofold understanding of folk art. With respect to the individual-creative notion, the terms can be helpful to suggest the meaning of folk art as a relative concept, whose reference point is academic art. In other words, they can assist us in recognizing the characteristics which distinguish the expressions of folk artists from the more formally disciplined and sophisticated work of the academy. Such terms are less helpful, however, when applied to the ethnic-traditional notion of folk art, where there is considerable technical refinement in the perpetuation and variation upon ancient themes, the repetition and recombination of a fixed vocabulary of decorative motifs. It is interesting, in this connection, to observe the aesthetic judgements of historians, students and collectors of folk art. A folk art object of the individual-creative type is likely to be praised for its amateur, or primitive qualities, while an example of ethnic-traditional folk art is valued precisely on opposite grounds, for its high degree of refinement.

We find ourselves confronted, then, with two distinct though related notions which we have called folk art. The ethnic-traditional nexus is the readily familiar one. With few exceptions, most persons are quick to acknowledge Pennsylvania German *fraktur* or Québec sugar-moulds as folk art. Not so easily classified, perhaps, are the many examples of individual-creative folk art, the products of unschooled artists in which specific cultural background is not always easily discerned. Nevertheless, certain prevailing characteristics continually make their appearance in discussions of this latter category. Among these are features having to do with the artwork itself. These include naive elements of technique and gaucheries of subject matter, faulty perspective, emphasis upon details at the expense of compositional coherence, archaic elements such as hierarchical scale to reflect the artist's sense of priorities rather than empirical realism, working with unsophisticated tools, use of unmixed colours and other approaches which would constitute an embarrassment to an academically trained artist. The work of the naive artist is often characterized by short cuts, used not so much as the solution to as the avoidance of one technical problem or another. An interesting example is the case of Saskatchewan artist Dmytro Stryjek (1899-   ), who owned frames too large for his pictures. Rather than reducing the size of the frames, he enlarged the paintings by adding pieces of cardboard upon which he painted an 'extension' of the original picture! Frequently, the composition of naive painting reveals evidence of a process of 'additive detail', a tendency to fill in extraneous space in the concern to 'complete' the work. This approach is strikingly apparent in the work of artists such as Anna Weber (1814-1888), Clarence Webster (c. 1900-   ) or Joseph Sleep (1914-1978), where background voids and even the space between legs of a horse are cluttered with flowers and other embellishments.

Despite significant variations of opinion, there are many shared assessments as to what constitutes the naive artist himself or herself. Setting aside social-economic and psychological factors, which probably have considerably less to do with the determination of the naive artist than is suggested in much romanticized literature on the subject, there are nonetheless certain qualities which are generally viewed as essential to the definition of the folk artist. One of these criteria is that he or she be self-taught. There are limits to this restriction, to be certain. A village blacksmith or rug-maker most surely learns from others, as does a fraktur artist. But the locus of teaching and learning is a highly localized one – from father to son, mother to daughter, village school-teacher to pupil, neighbour to neighbour. Such learning with its domestic or local confinement is far removed from the worldly-wise realm of the academy. Because of the limitations of the learning process, the naive artist seems generally not to 'improve' his technique except to a minimal degree. This characteristic of folk art has been described elsewhere in the claim that folk art gives the impression of continually beginning from the beginning.[3] Whereas the academic artist develops within the historical trend and possesses an informed awareness of the artistic past, the mainstream and contemporary directions, the naive artist is defined rather by his isolation from the trend. Rather than manifesting evidence of participation in the collective artist experience, the naive artist develops within the confined framework of his own limited and isolated experience. His 'style' is not schooled, but rather singular. In a sense, the naive artist stands outside history, as implied by the claim made for the artist Henri Rousseau, that he 'had no forerunners, and he could have no followers.'[4] Perhaps it is the gap between blissful ignorance and worldly knowledge which distinguishes Rousseau from his contemporary Utrillo, the latter working in the Montmartre environment of artists where he was able to master broad ranges of aesthetic discussion and join the development of professional art.[5]

There is inescapably to be acknowledged an ambiguous zone which separates folk art from academic art on the one hand, and from crafts on the other. Nevertheless, the present compendium is developed on the belief that a certain reasonable delineation of contours can be designated with reference to the criteria we have been discussing here. With these principles in mind, certain forms of artistic expression are placed rather tentatively within the framework at hand. Hence, although the present volume acknowledges the work of army engineers, naval draughtsmen and topographical artists, as well as academic artists sometimes reaching marginally into the realm of the naive, the discussion of each takes into account a rationale for their inclusion. The presence of such artists in certain Canadian folk art volumes has not been always convincing, and serves to create the confusing impression that virtually anything is folk art. There are special complexities also with respect to an uncritical including of Indian or Inuit art. Nowhere does there seem to be a more distressing confusion of the word 'primitive' than in cases where African or Indian masks are thrown into a jumbled discussion with amateur backyard artists. For the amateur artist, a work is perhaps to be considered primitive relative to the formal sophistication of a culture's high art. But in an African or Canadian Indian cultural group, the mask or totem *is* the high art. To place these works alongside naive whittlers and painters is to demean the highly-articulated and intellectualized process which produced the former.

Folk art in the present context is further distinguished from the craft-work that has become increasingly popular in recent years, represented in rigidly-patterned hooked rugs, liquid embroidery, molded ceramics and other crafts in which mechanical repetition and mass reproduction plays a central role.

The entries in the following pages, arranged alphabetically, represent an attempt to provide an encyclopedia of Canadian folk artists as presently known in existing publications, exhibitions and accessible information from museums, galleries and other institutions. To be certain, greater or lesser bio-graphical detail generally reflects a situation in which we have available uneven data concerning various individuals. Indeed, in some cases, little more is known of an artist than a single signed work from his or her hand.

Where the individual's role within a working definition of folk art is especially ambiguous, an effort is made to suggest a rationale for the inclusion of the artist in question. This is particularly the case with respect to draughtsmen, topographical artists and others who have sometimes been labeled 'provincial' artists (Harper, A People's Art, 1974), or concerning contemporary trained artists who have worked consciously within what might be termed a 'naive style'. Other tasks are posed by the matter of certain categories of artists in which there are so many practitioners as to make systematic inclusion within a single volume nearly impossible. Notable in this respect are decoy carvers and yard artists. In the former instance, the vast number of Canadian decoy makers is gradually being catalogued in such major works as the Kangas, Gates and Guyette volumes, along with several projects in progress, and the reader is referred to these sources for more extensive discussion. The present work includes many of these artists, particularly those whose work is already known from existing studies, exhibitions and catalogues. Respecting yard artists, the ephemeral nature of the art form makes systematic recording most difficult. Nevertheless, many such artists that have gained attention through such varied projects as the major Québec survey (Grosbois et al, 1974) and the Newfoundland exhibition (Flights of Fancy, 1983) are included, along with others reported by respondents or visited directly. It is hoped that by means of supplementary publications to be brought out at future times it will be possible to extend what must be in many respects a preliminary investigation of a rich field of exploration, and that through such supplements it will be possible to include further material on Canadian folk artists presently overlooked or yet to be discovered.

Allowing for vagueness at the outer perimeters, the present approach is grounded in the conviction that folk art is, in the end, recognizable and distinguishable in its essence. This possibility of so designating the field of enquiry has been perhaps most evocatively expressed in the observation of anthropologist Roger L. Welsch, describing the rolling hills of his farm in the American Plains. In noting the absence of clear boundaries separating hills from one another, he remarks, 'hills are defined not by their edges but by the middles.'[6] It is with a similar appreciation of the notion of substantial centres that we approach the phenomenon of folk art.

At the end of each descriptive entry there appears a listing of sources and collections in which information or art works may sometimes by consulted. The abbreviation *Ref* (reference) designates articles, books, chapters or other written sources, while *Inf* (information) indicates individuals who have provided data in interviews or by correspondence. *Coll* (collection) refers to museums, libraries, galleries, archives or other public institutions where the work of particular artists may be found.

[1] For a brief but succinct discussion, cf. Roger Cardinal, *Primitive Painters* (New York: St. Martin's Press, 1979), pp. 1-2.

[2] Ultimately, one might argue that all folk art is eventually derived from high art, in that the decorative motif associated with, say, 18th century European peasant culture, is distantly related to the official decorative embellishment of architecture, funerary monuments or other aspects of ancient Near Eastern civilization.

[3] David Larkin, *Innocent Art* (New York: Ballantine Books, 1974), p. 5.

[4] *Primitive Painting: An Anthology of the World's Naive Painters* (Zagreb: Spektar, 1981), p. 17.

[5] *Ibid.*, p. 17.

[6] Roger L. Welsch, 'Beating a Live Horse: Yet Another Note on Definitions and Defining', in Ian Quimby and Scott T. Swank, *Perspectives on American Folk Art* (New York: W.W. Norton & Company, 1980), p. 226.

Foreword

Throughout the world, folk art scholarship has grown dramatically in the past several years. Art historians, private collectors and museum curators have come to value their folk heritage and have brought ever greater awareness to the field through continued research, the presentation of numerous exhibitions and extensive publishing in both the popular and academic press.

In Canada, Michael Bird and Terry Kobayashi are pre-eminent scholars with tireless energy and admirable determination. Their investigations have led them to traverse the nation time and time again in their quest to identify the best of Canada's great folk art. With the keen eyes of art historians, they have discovered remarkable works of folk expression which they have organized into trail-blazing exhibitions, accompanied by important catalogues. They have published numerous books and many articles which have contributed significantly to the literature as well. A *Compendium of Canadian Folk Art* is the latest of their many impressive efforts. All of us who are intrigued with folk expression, whatever nation we live in, are grateful for the important contributions made by Terry Kobayashi and Michael Bird. Scholars and collectors have long waited for just such a concise and informative dictionary of folk art in Canada.

Dr. Robert Bishop
Director, Museum of American Folk Art

ABBOT, J. (active 1860s)
    Painter   Montréal, Québec
This artist is best known for a single oil painting, signed and dated (1863). A
genre picture, it is an inspired amateur depiction of a man and woman riding in a horse-drawn sleigh, against a landscape background of what appears
to be the St. Lawrence River and hills beyond.

Ref: Harper, A *People's Art*

ACKERMANN, GEORGE (active 1860s)
    Painter   Ontario
Most likely a resident of eastern Ontario, he is known for several watercolour scenes signed by or attributable to his hand. Most of these works
show Picton Harbour and other nearby places along the north shore of Lake
Ontario. His 1866 picture of Picton Harbour uses exaggerated perspective and
depth-of-field to suggest a village with wide, spacious streets, along which
move pedestrians and horse-drawn passenger vehicles, reflective of considerable commercial activity and personal prosperity.

Ref: Harper, *People's Art* (catalogue)
Coll: Bank of Montréal

AIDE-CRÉQUY, JEAN-ANTOINE (1746-1780)
    Painter   Québec City, Québec
Descended from a family of master masons, this painter produced numerous
religious works in oil. Many are recognizable as adaptations of European
prints and engravings, and some are considered to have been modeled after
early French painter Frère Luc (active in Canada 1670-1671). He is a strongly
academic painter; it is only with respect to occasionally awkward adaptations
from earlier sophisticated works that we can perceive a certain degree of
naivete in some paintings by the prolific Aide-Créquy.

Ref: Harper, *Painters and Engravers*
Coll: Episcopal Palace, Chicoutomi; Hôtel Dieu, Québec;
    Ursuline Convent, Québec

AINSLIE, H.F. (1803-1879)
    Painter   Québec and Ontario
A topographical landscape painter, Ainslie toured Canada with the British

Alexander, Hugh (1913-   ). *Prairie Landscape*. Oil on canvas: 1973.

Army during the period 1838-43. He sketched along the St. Lawrence, Chaudière, Rideau and Ottawa Rivers, producing finished watercolour landscapes which provided an accurate geographical record of places visited. In that his simplicity of detail owes as much to the economy of scientific necessity as to any lack of draughtsmanship competency, the placement of Ainslie within the category of folk or naive art is made with some tentativeness.

Ref: Harper, *Painters and Engravers*
Coll: Public Archives of Canada

Hugh Alexander
1973

AIREY, SIR RICHARD (1803-1881)
Painter   Ontario

This topographical landscape painter was stationed in Toronto, London and St. Thomas, Ontario, during the 1830s. He painted several sepia watercolour views of London and the St. Thomas districts while on his stay in Canada. Like H. F. Ainslie and other topographical artists, Airey's position within the definition folk painters is a marginal one at best.

Ref: Harper, Painters and Engravers
Coll: University of Western Ontario

AKINS, THOMAS BEAMISH (1809-1891)
Painter   Halifax, Nova Scotia
Born in Liverpool, England, Akins migrated to Canada as a young man. He
was admitted to the Nova Scotia bar in 1831. He was well-known as a local
historian and he published *History of Halifax* in 1849. Akins painted oil and
watercolour portraits, many of which were copied from portraits of Nova
Scotia historical figures, and after American painters, notably Smibert and
Copley. Occasional works indicate a degree of simplification in comparison
to prototypes used.

Ref: Harper, *Painters and Engravers*
Coll: King's College, Halifax

ALARY, ZACHARY (active mid-20th century)
Woodcarver   Lavaltrie, Québec
Alary's woodcarving may have been, like that of New Brunswick carver Art
Gallant, motivated partially by monetary prospects. From his home in the
Laurentians, he undoubtedly carved many pieces for amusement, but also
provided figures upon request for neighbours, friends, or persons answering
his advertising. An interesting example of his work is a standing nude
woman, carved for a patron who refused to accept it (as in the case of
George Cockayne, who carved a head for a neighbour's wife, only to have it
rejected). Although Alary may have been interested in carving from an early
time, it was in later years that he took up the pastime in earnest.

Inf: Patrick Laurette
Coll: Art Gallery of Nova Scotia

ALEXANDER, HUGH (1913-   )
Painter   Weyburn, Saskatchewan
A self-taught painter, Hugh Alexander first took up drawing after age 40. He
did not pursue the hobby in earnest until nearly 60, when he began to paint
oil pictures of nostalgic subjects. Depicting long-gone days of life on the
farms and in the villages of his Saskatchewan upbringing, he painted broad
landscapes, harvest scenes, village landmarks, and genre subjects, including
farm labour, domestic activities and glimpses of life in the Roaring Twenties
or Dirty Thirties. In contrast to some of his contemporaries, who produced
vertical pictures of trees, buildings and grain elevators, Hugh Alexander's
paintings are flat and horizontal in emphasis.

Anger, Ken (1905-1961). Canada Goose decoy. Painted wood: c. 1948.

Ref: artscanada (December, 1969); *artscanada* (October / November 1979);
    Grassroots Art; Seven Saskatchewan Artists
Coll: National Museum of Man (CCFCS); Saskatchewan Arts Board

ANDRESS, RAY (1889-1955)
    Decoy carver   Gananoque, Ontario
A boat-builder, hunter and decoy maker, he carved whistlers, canvasbacks,
bluebills and black ducks. His carved and painted works were so fine as to
inspire other makers along the St. Lawrence.

Ref: Gates, *Ontario Decoys*

ANDREWS, BILLY (active 1960s and after)
    Woodcarver   Bradford, Ontario
An orphan who came to Canada in the 1920s, Billy Andrews carved from
time to time in later life. He worked slowly and sporadically, hence the
number of works from his hand is not large. His carvings, generally of large
size, include various animals and birds, notably a stork, an eagle and domestic groups such as a mother pig and her piglets.

Ref: From the Heart; 'Twas Ever Thus
Coll: National Museum of Man (CCFCS)

ANGER, KEN (1905-1961)
    Decoy carver   Dunnville, Ontario
Generally respected as one of the masters of decoy carving, Anger made
many ducks and shorebirds found along the north shore of Lake Erie and in

the Grand River basin of southwestern Ontario. He is at times referred to as
the 'Rasp Master' because of his skill at texturing the surface of the decoy
with this carpenter's tool. Many of his ducks are distinguished by an unusual
blunt tail. His exceptionally refined painted finishes along with superb sculptural form make Anger decoys among the finest examples of the art.

Ref: Gates, Ontario Decoys; Kangas and Kangas, Decoys of North America; Kobayashi
    et al, Folk Treasures of Historic Ontario

'ANNAPOLIS CARVER' (active c. 1800-1820)
    Gravestone carver   Nova Scotia and New Brunswick
A stonecutter whose distinctively carved cherub-motif is found on tombstones in and around Annapolis Royal, Nova Scotia, and Saint John, New
Brunswick. This skillful craftsman used traditional design motifs known from
an earlier date in the British Isles and New England and worked possibly on
both shores of the Bay of Fundy.

Ref: Trask, Life How Short

ATKINSON, CHARLIE (1904-1977)
    Woodcarver   South Side, Cape Sable Island, Nova Scotia
A versatile craftsman, he made many birdhouses, small models, decoys,
decorative ducks, mechanical sculptures and yard ornaments. As a young
man, he carved or assembled miniature bobsleds, wheelbarrows and decoys.
In the late 1950s he turned to a variety of animals and yard art. Charlie gave
up carving in the 1970s as the result of a severe heart attack and stroke
which crippled his hand. His work is rather distinctive for the unusual spot-
ted painting technique which he developed.

Ref: Folk Art of Nova Scotia; From the Heart
Coll: Art Gallery of Nova Scotia; National Museum of Man (CCFCS)

AUDET, T. (active late 19th century)
    Painter   Québec
This amateur artist is most likely the painter of numerous scenes of shipping

Audet, T. (active late 19th century). Steamship *Québec*. Watercolour on
paper: late 19th century. Coll: National Museum of Man (CCFCS).

activity along the St. Lawrence River. A signed watercolour is of particular
interest because of its studied attention to minute details of the steamship
Québec, suggesting that the artist possessed first-hand acquaintance with the
technical fine points of such vessels. In addition to awkward depiction of
waves and land formations, overall composition is decidedly naive in that
the perspective lines of the ship are inconsistent with those of the fuller
landscape of which it is a part.

Ref: National Museum of Man Archives (CCFCS)
Coll: National Museum of Man (CCFCS)

AVANN, CLIFF (1891-   )
Decoy carver   Toronto, Ontario
Known by friends as 'the fastest decoy-maker in North America,' he earned
a reputation for his ability to produce a finished decoy in eight minutes. His
career began as a youthful hunter at Ashbridge's Bay when he decided to
make for himself the decoys he could not afford to buy. A plumber by
trade, Avann would use his spare time to make decoys, starting with a
bandsaw and finishing with a penknife. He achieved exceptional decorative
work using his own custom-mixed paints. He sold many decoys through
local sporting-goods stores and often carved birds upon request.

Ref: Gates, *Ontario Decoys; Star Weekly* (September 1964)

BACKMAN, CAPTAIN EDWIN (1872-1914)

Decoy carver   Lunenburg, Nova Scotia

Captain Backman was an off-shore fisherman and captain of a cargo schooner working out of Lunenburg. Although the number of decoys known to have been made by him is comparatively small (approximately 40), his work is of exceptionally high quality. His stylish mergansers, whistlers and scoters are marked by muted colour and strong flowing contours. Delicate bills, thin crests and intricate paint distinguish the mergansers. In later life he travelled widely to Newfoundland, Europe and the West Indies. In 1914 he set sail for the West Indies and was never heard from again.

Ref: Guyette and Guyette, *Decoys of Maritime Canada*

BAKER, JESSE (1888-1961)

Decoy carver   Trenton, Ontario

As a fireman in this southern Ontario community, Jesse Baker had to pursue decoy carving in what spare time he could find in evenings or on weekends. It is estimated that between 1930-1950 he produced some 3,000 decoys, which he sold to hunters in both Canada and the United States. He carved whistlers, black ducks, teal, pintails and other varieties.

Ref: Gates, *Ontario Decoys*

BAKER, S.C. (active c. 1890)

Painter   Aylmer, Ontario

It is believed that S.C. Baker was an itinerant artist in Elgin County who did oil paintings at the request of patrons wishing to show off prize farm animals. He is known in particular for a signed picture of a champion work horse which he painted in the Aylmer area.

Ref: National Museum of Man Archives (CCFCS)
Coll: National Museum of Man (CCFCS)

BALDWIN, ALMA (1895-1977)

Sculptor   Big Bay Point, Ontario

Living in York and Simcoe counties, Alma Baldwin immersed herself in artistic activity during severe illness endured between 1948-1952, when she made soft sculpture works of a strongly satirical nature, using nylon stockings, batting, cosmetics and even human hair. Her subjects are

Barbier, Sister Marie (active late 17th century). *The Christ Child.* Oil on
canvas: late 17th century. Coll: Sisters of the Congregation of Notre-Dame.

frequently drawn from mass media stereotypes and popular culture.

Ref: From the Heart
Coll: National Museum of Man (CCFCS)

BALLARD, OREN L. (active c. 1858-1869)
    Potter   St. John's, Québec and Cornwall, Ontario
An immigrant craftsman from the United States who had earlier operated
stoneware potteries in Vermont, Oren Ballard produced wares in Québec

Barbour, Carl (1908-   ). *Whaling Station, Safe Hr. B. Bay 1910.* Acrylic on canvas: 1977. Coll: National Museum of Man (CCFCS).

and Ontario. Many of his pieces feature decorative motifs in the form of flowers or other designs painted in blue slip against a clear glaze background.

Ref: Newlands, *Early Ontario Potters;* Webster, *Early Canadian Pottery*
Coll: Royal Ontario Museum (Sigmund Samuel Canadiana Collection)

BANKS, WALLY (active 1970 and after)
    Woodcarver   Mount Hanley, Nova Scotia
Wally Banks had been an active farmer near Mount Hanley until he was forced by a heart attack in 1970 to give up such strenuous labour. Always an avid collector of bottles, insulators and other found items, he began to fill his shelves with his handiwork. His carvings include horses, cats, dogs, miniature furniture and other subjects, many of which have been bought by visitors from the United States, England and across Canada.

Ref: Peter Day, 'Roadside Attractions'

BARBIER, SISTER MARIE (c. 1663-1739)
Painter   Montréal, Québec

Sister Marie Barbier reputedly joined Marguerite Bourgeoys (1620-1700), founder of the Congregation of Notre-Dame. According to tradition, her painting of *The Christ Child* had been placed over the ovens, thereby preventing the burning of loaves of bread which were baked there daily. Her oil paintings are generally of religious subjects.

Ref: Harper, *A People's Art*
Coll: Congregation of Notre-Dame, Montréal

BARBOUR, CAPTAIN CARL (1908-   )
Painter   Newtown, Bonavista Bay, Newfoundland

An active seaman, engaged in whaling and sealing, Carl Barbour turned to painting upon his retirement in 1974. His acrylic paintings emphasize the sea and scenes drawn from memory. His compositions tend to be not so much realistic as decorative, with details such as boats or whales appearing too large for the landscapes or contexts in which they are placed.

Ref: 'Folk Art in Canada' (Clinton, New York); *From the Heart*
Coll: National Museum of Man (CCFCS)

BARIBEAU, WILFRID (1893-   )
Woodcarver   St-Léon, Maskinongé County, Québec

A highly diversified carver, Wilfrid Baribeau has created a broad range of birds and animals. Some are carved and assembled as groupings on whirligigs, or wind-toys. His specialty is that of crucifixion and biblical scenes carved and constructed inside glass bottles.

Ref: les patenteux de Québec

BARTER, MARTIN (1914-   )
Yard artist   Mainland, Port au Port Peninsula, Newfoundland

Recently retired from long years of work as a fisherman and house-builder, Martin Barter uses his leisure time for the decoration of his house and yard in this tiny coastal village. He created a yard environment of found materials, including machinery, appliances, fishing floats and stones cemented together to form walls and towers. To give colour, everything is painted red or white.

Ref: Flights of Fancy

Bauman, Joseph D. (1815-1899). Fraktur drawing. Watercolour
on paper: 1848.

BARTON, IRA B. (active 1851-1871)
   Painter   Demorestville, Ont.
In the 1850s Ira B. Barton advertised himself as a 'house and fancy painter' at
Demorestville. He is known to have done some oil paintings of genre subjects, notably a work adapted from an illustration in the highly popular Harriet Beecher Stowe book *Uncle Tom's Cabin*. This particular painting reveals the
artist's naivete of perspective and proportion in its sincere effort to follow
conventions of 18th-century French landscape painting.

Ref: Harper, A *People's Art*
Coll: Upper Canada Village

BAUMAN, JOSEPH D. (1815-1899)
   Fraktur artist   Waterloo County, Ontario
A Mennonite farmer in the Pennsylvania German countryside of Waterloo

County, Joseph Bauman proved himself highly capable in calligraphy and decorative drawing associated with the Pennsylvania folk art tradition. From the 1840s until the end of his life he produced numerous pen-and-ink and watercolour drawings for his family and relatives. He also executed decorated texts and family registers for the bibles of neighbouring families. Frequently he made use of commercially-printed Pennsylvania birth and baptismal certificates, from which he extracted flowers, hearts, birds and other motifs, placing them in new contexts.

Ref: Michael Bird, *Ontario Fraktur;* Michael Bird and Terry Kobayashi, A *Splendid Harvest*
Coll: Doon Pioneer Village and Heritage Museum; Joseph Schneider Haus Museum

BEAUCHEMIN, MATHIAS
Decoy carver   Vaudreuil, Québec
In the tradition of refined Québec craftsmanship, Mathias Beauchemin's decoys are meticulously carved, with deep and precise details throughout. He produced many varieties of ducks and other birds for himself and hunters along the St. Lawrence just east of Montréal.

Ref: Marsil Museum, *The Judas Birds*

BEAUDOIN, ANNA (active c. 1900)
Painter, sketch artist   St-Henri-de-Lévis, Québec
While little is known about the life of this amateur artist, there survives from her hand a signed picture of Québec City. It is a hand-drawn and coloured aerial view, depicting houses, trees and roads in faulty perspective.

Ref: Harper, A *People's Art*

BEAVER, JOHN (active late 19th century)
Painter   Brantford area, Ontario
James Beaver was raised on the Six Nations Reserve along the lower Grand River. Late in life he produced numerous oil paintings, principally landscapes. His sources appear to include lithographs and even calendar pictures. His rendering of perspective, as well as proportion, reveals a naive approach to compositional problems. Several of his pictures are extremely charming in their simplicity.

Ref: Kobayashi et al, *Folk Treasures of Historic Ontario*

BELBIN, LOUISE (1898-   )

Rug maker   Grand Bank, Newfoundland

28 Operating a confectionary in Grand Bank, Mrs. Belbin began to do rug making as her children grew older, to while away time when her husband was at sea. After his death she devoted all her spare time to 'matting', producing both geometric rugs and rugs featuring representational images such as ducks, cats and moose.

Ref: *The Fabric of Their Lives*

BELL, LYNN (1938-   )

Woodcarver   Kingston, Ontario

An amateur whittler and carver, he has made numerous animals, birds and weathervanes.

Ref: McKendry, *Folk Art*

BELLEFONTAINE, WALTER (1914-   )

Woodcarver   Chezzetcook, Halifax Co. Nova Scotia

Throughout his life, Walter has worked in a rope factory, for the railroad, as a mason and as an apprentice to an Italian marble carver employed by churches in Halifax. After retirement, he has made a number of large carvings with cloth covered bodies. These include a couple of giant MacAskills, a fisherman and a mermaid. A few early pieces had composition heads and hands. In later life he has been forced to give up carving due to poor health.

Inf: Chris Huntington

BERGERON, GASTON (1922-   )

Yard artist, woodcarver   Laval, Fabre County, Québec

Inspired by pictures in newspapers and magazines, he decided to create a full circus in miniature, making animals, performers and carriages on a scale of one inch to the foot. In all he has carved or constructed more than 3,000 pieces. His 'parade' was shown in 1967 at the Man and His World exhibition in Montréal.

Ref: *les patenteux du Québec*

Birrell, Ebenezer (1810-1888). *Good Friends*. Oil on canvas: mid-19th century.
Coll: Art Gallery of Hamilton.

BERNARD, EUGÉNE (1910-   )
  Woodcarver   St-André-Avellin, Québec
A whittler and carver, he made a large number of Calvaries, or crucifixion-
scenes, constructed inside glass bottles. His first such creation was made at
the age of 14. After assembling the crucifixion scene, he would fill the bottle
with water, causing the wood to swell. His largest Calvary was made in 1933;
the smallest in 1980.

Ref: National Museum of Man Archives (CCFCS)
Col: National Museum of Man (CCFCS)

BETTS, SPENCE H. (active 1883-1886)
  Potter   Tillsonburg, Ontario
Working in partnership with William Gray, Jr., he was engaged in making
stoneware as well as Rockingham wares. A number of pieces from this pot-

tery, made during the Betts tenure, are distinguished by blue-glazed floral decorative motifs.

Ref: Newlands, *Early Ontario Potters*

BIERNSTIHL, ADAM (1825-1899)
    Potter   Lexington and Bridgeport, Ontario
The Biernstihls emigrated from Germany to Canada, settling in Waterloo County in 1853. From approximately 1860 to 1899, Adam Biernstihl made utilitarian earthenware vessels for the local German community. Many of his wares are identifiable by distinctive blue or green decorative glazing. For his own immediate family he made numerous specialty pieces such as bird-toys, banks and a large bowl for his daughter, featuring two chickens primitively drawn in green slip against the yellow base.

Ref: Bird and Kobayashi, A *Splendid Harvest;* Newlands, *Early Ontario Potters*
Coll: National Museum of Man (History Division); Royal Ontario Museum
    (Sigmund Samuel Canadiana Collection); Joseph Schneider Haus Museum

BIRRELL, EBENEZER (1801-1888)
    Painter   Pickering, Ontario
Born in Scotland, Birrell emigrated to Canada in 1834, settling at the village of Pickering, east of Toronto. He was a well-educated man, becoming a local superintendent of education and president of the Pickering Agricultural Society. He was known locally as an amateur painter, and he produced oil portraits and landscapes, as well as watercolour landscapes of English scenery. His paintings of domestic animals against cultivated farm backgrounds recall the serenity of the American Quaker painter Edward Hicks.

Ref: Harper, *Painters and Engravers;* Harper, A *People's Art*
Coll: Art Gallery of Hamilton; Art Gallery of Windsor

BLAKE, SARA M. (1864-1933)
    Painter   Pincher Creek, Alberta
Born in Galway, Scotland, Mrs. Blake came to her brother Frank's ranch, The Deer Horn, near Pincher Creek, around 1880. She remained in Alberta for the remainder of her life. She was a self-taught artist, and is known by a

Bolduc, Blanche (1907-   ). Québec rural scene. Oil on canvas: mid-20th century. Coll: National Museum of Man (CCFCS).

signed watercolour painting, 'Deer Horn Ranch', which she executed in 1889.

Ref: Glenbow Collects
Coll: Glenbow Museum

BLOUIN, ADÉLARD (1895-   )
Yard artist, model maker   Montréal, Québec
From his days of working for the Canadian Pacific Railway, he became familiar with the many details which are featured in his miniature train and replica of a village which he designated 'Blouinville'. For his train setting he cut out and constructed miniature houses, stores and churches.

Ref: les patenteux du Québec

BOCK, JACOB (1798-1867)
Potter   Freeport, Waterloo County, Ontario
Jacob Bock emigrated as a young man from Lancaster County, Pennsylvania,

to live at the farm of his uncle, Christian Reichert, at Freeport along the Grand River. For a brief period he produced pottery for the local Mennonite community, with known pieces dating from 1822 to 1825. Using molds for decorative effect, he made several unique earthenware jars with elaborate details, including faces or masks and figures marked 'S. Ambrosious'. After his brief pottery career, he took up farming and later became a deacon in the Blenheim Mennonite Church.

Ref: Bird and Kobayashi, A *Splendid Harvest*; Newlands, *Early Ontario Potters*
Coll: Royal Ontario Museum (Sigmund Samuel Canadiana Collection)

BOEHLER, VALENTINE (1852-1876)
    Potter   Egmondville, Huron County, Ontario
After arriving in Canada at mid-century, Valentine Boehler established himself in the pottery enterprise in Huron County, producing utilitarian yellow earthenwares. By late 19th century he was introducing decorative treatment on jars, flower pots and other pieces in the form either of applied floral motifs or of painted blue designs reminiscent of those more customarily associated with stoneware decoration in New England and eastern Canada.

Ref: Bird and Kobayashi, A *Splendid Harvest*; Newlands, *Early Ontario Potters*
Coll: Royal Ontario Museum (Sigmund Samuel Canadiana Collection);
    National Museum of Man (History Division)

BOLDUC, BLANCHE (1907-   )
    Painter   Baie-St-Paul, Charlevoix County, Québec
One of several members of this artistic family who produced paintings of the Charlevoix region during the 1930s. She painted many oil renditions of local events, processions, church-going and village scenes. Drawing upon her childhood memories, she has expressed a yearning for an ideal past, saying, 'For me, painting is a means of recalling beautiful things of the past, a time when life was much more beautiful.'

Ref: *From the Heart*; Harper, *People's Art* (Catalogue); *Images de Charlevoix 1784-1950*;
    Morgan, 'Folk Painters of Charlevoix'
Coll: Dominion Gallery, Montréal; Musée du Québec; National Museum of
    Man (CCFCS)

BOLDUC, YVONNE (1905-   )
    Painter, woodcarver   Baie-St-Paul, Charlevoix County, Québec
Having learned the art of woodworking from her father, a carpenter, she is
rather exceptional in being one of few known Canadian women woodcarvers. She is best known, however, for her many paintings, done in oil,
depicting farm and village life, especially around the Bouchard ancestral
home in Charlevoix County. Before 1923 she painted or carved only for her
own amusement, but in that year a new road was built in front of the
house, bringing many visitors and tourists. Some of her subject matter was
drawn from literature, folklore and radio programmes, notably 'Un homme
et son péchée', 'Maria Chapdelaine', and 'Le curé du village' by Robert Cho-
quette, describing the traditional life of French Canada. Yvonne has
described her 'true' perspective and realism in distinction from the 'naive'
quality of the work of her sister Blanche.

Ref: From the Heart; Harper, People's Art (Catalogue); Images de Charlevoix 1784-
    1950); Morgan, 'Folk Painters of Charlevoix'
Coll: Dominion Gallery, Montréal; Musée du Québec; National Museum of
    Man (CCFCS)

BOLLIVAR, SAMUEL (1884-   )
    Painter   Lunenburg County, Nova Scotia
Born at Rhodes Corner and later living at Dayspring, he began painting after
his retirement from a strenuous life of shipyard labour and fishing. His paintings were usually given to family members or hung on the porch for his
own pleasure. Most of his subjects were related to seafaring.

Ref: Folk Art of Nova Scotia; From the Heart
Coll: National Museum of Man (CCFCS)

BOSSY, WALTER J. (1899-   )
    Collage artist   Montréal, Québec
Son of a Swiss mother and Polish father, he was born in Jaslo, Poland. He
came to Canada in 1923 'for adventures', preceding the arrival of his wife and
children by eight months. His wife was Ukrainian. He claims to have been
unable to speak a word of English, but eventually became a teacher at a
boys' college in Yorktown, Saskatchewan. His 'Allegorical Structure' contains
strong moral pronouncements against the excesses of capitalism, and a plea

for giving greater attention to the spiritual nature of man. He voiced his dislike for the 'Man and His World' exhibition in Montréal, saying that it failed to include God and the universe.

Ref: National Museum of Man Archives (CCFCS)

BOUCHARD, ARTHUR (1930-   )
   Yard artist, woodcarver   Baie-St-Paul, Charlevoix County, Québec
A brick-layer by trade, he used his leisure-time hours to carve and paint many small animals, birds, fish and still-life scenes of fruit, nuts and vegetables. Many of these works were to become elements of a yard 'environment', while others were kept as free-standing pieces in the house.

Ref: les patenteux du Québec

BOUCHARD, MARIE-CECILE (1920-1973)
   Painter   Baie-St-Paul, Charlevoix County, Québec
One of three sisters who were to become well-known naive artists, Marie-Cecile's artistic activity was initiated at the age of 18 when she learned rudiments of painting from her older sister Simone Mary Bouchard. She painted for a brief period before she entered a convent in 1947, the Sisters of Sainte Antonniennes de Marie. Her simple oil paintings depict the Bouchard mill home, fields and forests. She continued to paint at the convent, although on a reduced scale, until shortly before her death in 1973.

Ref: arts populaires (Catalogue); A Dictionary of Canadian Artists; Images de Charlevoix;
   Morgan, 'Folk Painters of Charlevoix'
Coll: Dominion Gallery, Montréal; Musée du Québec

BOUCHARD, SIMONE MARY (1912-1945)
   Painter   Baie-St-Paul, Charlevoix County, Québec
Always revealing evidence of artistic ability, Simone Mary Bouchard first made hooked rugs at her mill home near Baie-St-Paul, selling them to visitors and tourists. She quickly proved herself a talented, if completely self-taught, painter, and was at the centre of the activity of the group of 'Charlevoix folk painters' who made their appearance in the 1930s. She painted farm and village subjects, horses grazing in fields, domestic events and cheerful interior scenes. She also painted several religious subjects. One of her best-known paintings, The Three Kings, shows the biblical figures intermingled with her

Bouchard, Simone Mary (1912-1945). *The Three Kings*. Oil on canvas: 1930s.

own family in the Bouchard living-room. This charming picture was featured on one of the 1984 Canadian Christmas postage stamps.

Ref:arts populaires (Catalogue); Harper, *People's Art;* (Catalogue), *Images de Charlevoix 1784-1950*; Lessard, *l'art traditionnel au Québec*; Morgan, 'Folk Painters of Charlevoix'
Coll: Dominion Gallery, Montréal; Musée du Québec; National Museum of Man (CCFCS)

BOUDREAU, DONALD
Woodcarver   St. Bernard, Nova Scotia
Mr. Boudreau started his adult life as a lumberjack in this small community in Digby County and later turned his hand to fishing. In later years he became a woodworker in a mill and then owner of his own lumberyard. During the winters after 1974 he pursued an active hobby of woodcarving. He made a variety of subjects, including whirligigs, seagulls, animals and several human figures. Some of his subjects, such as a life-size female bather in a two-piece bathing suit, are inspired by pictures in newspapers and maga-

zines. He also took up painting, producing numerous pictures of landscapes and flowers.

Inf: Chris Huntington *Ref: From the Heart;* Waddington's catalogue
(June 15-17, 1980)
Coll: National Museum of Man (CCFCS)

BOURGAULT, ANDRÉ (active 1930s to mid-20th century)
    Woodcarver   St-Jean-Port-Joli, Québec
A member of the famed Bourgault family of woodcarvers, he carved many works individually or in collaboration with his brothers Médard and Jean-Julien. The three craftsmen operated a sculpture workshop at St-Jean-Port-Joli, an enterprise which was to be continued by descendants to the present day. He carved religious figures and settings, animals, secular human figures, tableaux depicting religious events or daily anecdotes.

Ref: Canadian Geographic (December 1952); *From the Heart*
Coll: Church of Saint-Jean-Port-Joli; National Museum of Man (CCFCS)

BOURGAULT, L. (active early 20th century)
    Woodcarver   Québec
An unidentified woodcarver, who made and signed a finely-shaped canoe cup whose handle is elaborately fashioned in the form of a beaver on a branch.

Ref: 'Folk Art in Canada' (catalogue)
Coll: National Museum of Man (CCFCS)

BOURGAULT, MÉDARD (1897-1967)
    Woodcarver   St-Jean-Port-Joli, Québec
The most prominent of the family of outstanding wood sculptors, Médard's first carved work was a piece of furniture, a bookcase whose doors and drawers he embellished with a proliferation of vines, flowers, trees and beaver, made in 1918. Best known for his religious subjects, he carved his first crucifix in 1921. Throughout his life he produced an enormous quantity and variety of sculptural works, including Christ-figures, madonnas, Last-Supper scenes, and Stations of the Cross. Secular subjects include habitants, musicians, dancers and various tableaux depicting scenes from Québec history and folklore. In 1940 he and his brother Jean-Julien initiated a course in wood sculp-

Boutilier, Ralph (1906-   ). Seagull and Pollock. Painted metal: 1975. Coll: National Museum of Man (CCFCS).

ture at their studio, continued by other family members to the present.

Ref: Lessard, *l'art traditionnel au Québec;* Saint-Pierre, *Médard Bourgault, Sculpteur*
Coll: Church of Saint-Jean-Port-Joli; McCord Museum; Musée du Québec;
    National Museum of Man (CCFCS)

BOURGAULT, JEAN-JULIEN (active 1930s to mid-20th century)
    Woodcarver   St-Jean-Port-Joli, Québec
A capable carver who, along with his brothers André and Médard, operated
the Bourgault family workshop for many years at St-Jean-Port-Joli. Following
the Second World War, when the sculpture school was temporarily closed,
classes were begun again by André and Jean-Julien, keeping alive the ancient
tradition of Québec figural carving.

Ref: Saint-Pierre, *Médard Bourgault, Sculpteur*

BOUTILIER, RALPH (1906-   )
    Woodcarver, builder   Milton, Queens County, Nova Scotia
In his youth he held employment for several years on a tugboat. Skills

Brandt, William (active 1860s). *Establishment of James Young, Esquire at Tracadie.*
Watercolour on paper: 1862. Coll: Old Manse Library

developed during this period in mechanics; carpentry and painting were
later to serve him well when he took up his hobby of making whirligigs and
lawn ornaments. He made a number of variations of an unusual device, a
large bird whose tail feathers rotate in the wind, providing movement
which forces the wings to flap up and down and the beak to open and
close. He primarily thought of himself as a painter of scenery and marine-
related subjects but found his fame grew much greater as a carver of life-
sized figures.

Ref: Folk Art of Nova Scotia; From The Heart
Coll: National Museum of Man (CCFCS); AGNS

BRANDT, WILLIAM (active 1860s)
    Painter   New Brunswick
Born in Germany, he arrived around mid-century in Canada, after which
time he became a New Brunswick school teacher at Tracadie. He is known
for his watercolour paintings of farms and views along New Brunswick's
North Shore, particularly in the Newcastle area.

Ref: Harper, *A People's Art*
Coll: Old Manse Library, Newcastle, New Brunswick; York-Sunbury Historical
    Society, Fredericton

BRAUN, HELLA KLASSEN (1925-)
  Doll-maker   Kitchener, Ontario
Born at Osterwich in the Ukraine, she moved in 1943 to Germany where she
lived until 1948, at which time she emigrated to Canada. In 1950 she married
Peter Braun, whom she had met at their baptism in 1946. She is well-known
as a maker of cloth-wrapped wire dolls, a technique which she learned from
her youth in the Ukraine. Her 1953 Nativity scene was eventually to be given
prominence by its appearance on the 1982 Canadian Christmas postage stamp.

Ref: Nancy-Lou Patterson, Swiss-German and Dutch-German Mennonite Traditional Art
    in the Waterloo Region, Ontario

BRICKER, BENJAMIN (active 1890s)
  Violin-maker   Washington, Oxford County, Ontario
A reclusive Mennonite woodcarver, he made numerous musical instru-
ments, some of which were used at local barn dances in Oxford and
Waterloo counties.

Ref: Nancy-Lou Patterson, Mennonite Traditional Arts

BROKENSHIRE, SILAS (active late 19th century)
  Woodcarver, builder   Fenelon Falls, Ontario
An amateur whittler and carver, he is known for a number of carved
animals and rocking horses.

Ref: 'Twas Ever Thus

BROOKS, JOHN (1879-1962)
  Decoy carver   Freeland, Prince Edward Island
Brooks was a carpenter at Freeland, as well as engaged in occasional farming
and working as a guide for sportsmen visiting the island. When the use of
live geese as decoys was outlawed, he drew upon his woodworking abilities
to make his own models. Many of Brooks' decoys possess a rustic quality,
with whittle marks evident. He made many geese and ducks, the latter in
both floater and stick-up forms. In the 1950s he carved several winged teal,
based upon Québec models which had been given to him earlier. Most
Brooks decoys bear a 'J.B.' stamp on the underside.

Ref: Guyette and Guyette, Decoys of Maritime Canada

BROUSSEAU EMELIE (1843-1939)

Rug-maker   St-Simon, Bagot County, Québec

She was born at the village of St-Simon, in what was at the time a virgin forest wilderness. Among various rugs which she is believed to have made, one of the best-known is an example with a pictorial representation of the homestead of the Lavalee de la Richelierre Brousseau family of St-Simon.

Ref: National Museum of Man Archives (CCFCS)
Coll: National Museum of Man (CCFCS)

BROWN, A. (active 1820s)

Painter   Québec City, Québec

Little is known of the life and work of this capable artist outside a small number of signed or attributed watercolour and gouache paintings of daily life in the Québec City region.

Ref: Harper, People's Art (catalogue)
Coll: National Gallery of Canada

BROWN, ERSKINE (1892-   )

Woodcarver, builder   Thornbury, Ontario

A retired farmer living in the South Georgian Bay area, he began woodcarving as a hobby at age 13. He was inspired in particular by the whittling of a prison inmate who had carved a chain from a broom handle, a feat which Erskin was determined to match. Following the death of his wife in 1967, he devoted countless lonely hours carving miniatures of people and making tiny replicas of farm implements remembered from his youth.

Ref: From the Heart
Coll: National Museum of Man (CCFCS)

BROWN, MISS (active c. 1890)

Painter   Glenmore District, Alberta

She is known principally for her oil painting of the log home of her brother Osborne Brown (1867-1941), located near the Elbow River.

Ref: Harper, Peoples's Art (catalogue)
Coll: Glenbow Museum

Bruce, Douglas (active mid-to-late 19th century). *Sam Tawse*. Painted wood: c. 1858.

BROWNSCOMBE, WILLIAM (active 1852-1881)
Potter   Peterborough, Ontario
He made earthenwares at his establishment at Peterborough, producing a
relatively diverse range of utilitarian storage wares and picture frames, as
well as several decorated specialty pieces. In partnership with his son-in-law,
Frank Goodfellow, he briefly made decorated stoneware between 1878-1881.

Ref: Newlands, *Early Ontario Potters*

BRUCE, DOUGLAS (active mid-19th century)
Sculptor   Guelph, Ontario
Comparatively little is known about the life of this highly competent woodcarver who may have been something of an itinerant craftsman. He is
remembered according to family tradition as a neighbour who was commissioned to carve a store figure for the Tawse shoe business in Guelph. In 1858
he produced a highly expressive figure in the form of an impish leprechaun,
with outstretched hands to display shoes. This charming store figure stood at
the door of the Tawse Shoe Store for many years after it was carved in 1858,
and an engraved version greeted readers of the *Guelph Mercury* into the 1870s.

Ref: Kobayashi et al, *Folk Treasures of Historic Ontario*

BRUCE, J. (active 1890s)
Painter   Huron County, Ontario
He is known for an oil painting depicting a farmstead in Huron County.

Ref: Harper, *Painters and Engravers*; Harper, *A People's Art*; *From the Heart*
Coll: National Museum of Man (CCFCS)

BRYANTON, STACY (1920-   )
Decoy carver   Kensington, Prince Edward Island
As with many decoy makers, it can be said that Stacy Bryanton's work
evolved in response to growing demand. His first birds were somewhat
crude, often having an unfinished appearance. This is particularly apparent in
the unrefined carving and in various shortcuts used, such as the insertion of
screws for eyes. In later years he became more concerned with accuracy,
producing elaborately carved field geese, mostly feeders and sleepers. He is
estimated to have made more than 500 decoys, depicting geese and flying
geese, as showpieces. Most of his decoys are painted or stamped 'S.B.'
on the bottom.

Buck, William (active c. 1840). Detail from *View of Penetanguishene*. Graphite and oil on canvas: c. 1840. Coll: National Gallery of Canada.

Ref: Guyette and Guyette, *Decoys of Maritime Canada*

BUCK, WILLIAM (active c. 1840)
    Painter   Central Ontario
Little is known about the artist, although several signed oil paintings testify to his considerable skill in depicting landmarks around Georgian Bay. A notable work is a picture of the *Gore*, the first passenger steamer on the upper Great Lakes, shown as it arrives at Penetanguishene.

Ref: Harper, *Painters and Engravers*; Harper, *People's Art* (catalogue)
Coll: National Gallery of Canada

BURGARD, FERDINAND (active 1870-1910)
    Potter   Egmondville, Huron County, Ontario
Born in Alsace, Burgard migrated to Canada in 1870. Joining his uncle, Valentine Boehler, he assisted at and eventually took over the Huron Pottery in 1900. He is known for numerous distinctive miniature earthenware jugs or whimseys whose inscriptions commemorate special events or individuals.

Ref: Newlands, *Early Ontario Potters*

BURLEIGH BROTHERS (ED, NORM, CLARENCE) (1900-1976)
　　Decoy carvers　　　　　　　　　　　　　　　　Toronto, Ontario
The three Burleigh brothers are important members of what is sometimes
called a 'Toronto school' of decoy carvers. They hunted at Ashbridges Bay,
where they built boats for sportsmen. Clarence was the major carver in the
group, although for the three brothers decoy-making was a joint venture.

Ref: Gates, Ontario Decoys

BURNS, JAMES R. (active 1879-1881)
　　Potter　　　　　　　　　　　　　　　　　　　　Toronto, Ontario
Born in County Tyrone, Ireland, where he had operated a pottery, Burns
opened a stoneware firm in Toronto in partnership with an Irish compatriot,
William J. Campbell. During the brief career of the pottery, Burns and
Campbell produced wares with blue floral decoration.

Ref: Newlands, Early Ontario Potters

BURT, LEONARD (1928-　　)
　　Painter　　　　　　　　　　　　　　　　Bonne Bay, Newfoundland
This self-taught artist was born at Port Saunders, on the West Coast. He has
spent most of his life in the Bonne Bay area. In later life he moved to St.
John's, working in an institution and confined to a wheelchair. His first work
– a horse in a landscape, painted on top of a wooden tea chest – was done at
age 13. His major works reflect earlier days of work on Canadian National
Coaster Steamers, or are panoramic views of Newfoundland's West Coast
and Northern Peninsula.

Ref: 'Folk Images '77' (Memorial University Art Gallery catalogue)

CALDWELL, MRS. ELSIE (active mid-19th century)
　　Painter　　　　　　　　　　　　　　　　　　　　Perth, Ontario
Known for a reverse painting on glass, entitled 'Castle and Bridge', she was
among those amateur artists who contributed to this popular form of
expression during much of the 19th century.

Ref: National Museum of Man Archives (Thomas Lackey file) (CCFCS)

CALDWELL, HARVEY (1930-   )
    Wood carver   Hampton Beach Road, Annapolis Co., Nova Scotia
Harvey is a middle-aged pensioner with a large family. He has worked as
both a woodsman and carpenter. When he finds time for his work, which
has been going on for perhaps 15 years or more, he likes to make buck
heads with real antlers and fish on plaques. He has made at least one life-
sized prone woman bather.

Inf: Chris Huntington

CAMERON, A. (active c. 1840)
    Painter   Québec City, Québec
An amateur watercolour artist and caricaturist serving in the British Army
stationed in Canada, he is known for a lithographed painted with watercolour, entitled A *Canadian Gentleman Going to a Frolic.*

Ref: Harper, A *People's Art*
Coll: Public Archives of Canada

CAMPBELL, COLIN (active c. 1897-1902)
    Gravestone carver   Inverness County, Nova Scotia
A late craftsman in an age dominated by mass-produced commercial gravestones, Colin Campbell carved unique motifs and configurations. His designs
include handshakes, flanking willows and blossoms.

Ref: Trask, *Life How Short*

CAMPBELL, D. (active c. 1885)
    Painter   Brockville, Ontario
Campbell was a soldier and self-taught painter. He did oil paintings of battle
scenes during the 1885 Canadian militia campaign against the Métis nation.
Although he may have used lithographs for sources, his use of colour, perspective and rendering of human figures is clearly of his own inspiration.

Ref: From the Heart
Coll: National Museum of Man(CCFCS)

CAMPBELL, WILLIAM J. (active c. 1877-c. 1885)
Potter   Brantford and Toronto, Ontario
Campbell was one of numerous Irish-born craftsmen who became accomplished stoneware artists in Canada. After his migration to Ontario, he worked at the Brantford stoneware factory from 1877-79 before joining James R. Burns in partnership in Toronto from 1879-1881. He returned to Brantford, working there for several years. He produced wares decorated with cobalt blue flower designs.

46

Ref: Newlands, Early Ontario Potters

CANNING, BERNIE (active mid-20th century and after)
Woodcarver   Simcoe County, Ontario
He has carved a highly diverse range of subjects in softwood. In particular he has carved various human figures, sometimes standing individually, other times in groups. Among his major carvings are a larger-than-life Indian chief, a three-man hillbilly band and various tableaux depicting light or humorous moments from daily life.

Ref: Waddington's catalogue (November 9-11, 1981)

CARBONNEAU, P. (active 1880s and later)
Painter   Québec City and Lévis, Québec
A St. Lawrence River captain residing in Lévis, he did large watercolour paintings, particularly of ships and ferries which continually plied the St. Lawrence River. His pictures are characterized by a strong linear quality, with clearly defined ships painted in light colours against an immense field of blue water and sky.

Ref: Harper, Painters and Engravers; Harper, A People's Art
Coll: McCord Museum; National Museum of Man (CCFCS)

CARON, PAUL EMILE (active mid-20th century and after)
Woodcarver   Québec
He carved many figures for display in his yard along the St. Lawrence Seaway. A number of his works are larger-than-life in size, particularly his carvings of fishermen and other human figures.

Ref: Waddington's catalogue (June 21-22, 1982)

Cauchon, Robert (1916-1969). *The Bread Oven*. Watercolour on paper: 1938.

CARRIÈRE, M. (active c. 1880-1900)
Painter   Lévis, Québec

Believed to have painted several vignettes of Québec life, he is particularly known for an oil picture showing winter woodcutting and other labour in the farmland along the south shore of the St. Lawrence. Landscape and distant houses provided a backdrop for a conversation and anecdotal subject matter in the foreground.

Ref: Harper, *People's Art* (catalogue)
Coll: McCord Museum

CARROLL, BARBARA (1952-   )
Painter   Toronto, Ontario

Born in Toronto, she studied natural science at the University of Toronto. She soon became well-known for her work as an illustrator, contributing to many publications, including *Homemakers Magazine, Better Homes and Gardens* and *City Magazine*. By 1980 she began to do oil paintings in a naive manner, depicting streets, houses and familiar buildings in Toronto. She exhibited her work in the Toronto Primitives Show at the Market Gallery in winter, 1984. She should be considered not a folk artist so much as a professional artist who in the early 1980s began to paint in a consciously 'primitive' style.

Ref: Toronto Primitives
Coll: Toronto Tours, Inc.

CAUCHON, ROBERT (active 1930s)(1916-1969)
    Painter   Charlevoix County, Québec
A member of the community of 'Folk Painters of Charlevoix', he depicted simple contemporary or past glimpses of domestic life in the vicinity, as in his watercolour paintings of women baking bread in outdoor ovens, persons on snowshoe outings and other subjects.

Ref: Harper, A *People's Art*
Coll: Dominion Gallery, Montréal

CHAMBERS, TOM (1860-1948)
    Decoy carver   Wallaceburg, Ontario
One of the best-known of southwestern Ontario carvers, he was active at the turn of the century as manager of the St. Clair Flats Shooting Club in this community east of Windsor. He made both solid- and hollow-body decoys which sold for as high as the remarkable price of $75 per dozen in the 1930s.

Ref: Gates, Ontario Decoys

CHAMPAGNE, NOE J. (1919-   )
    Rug-maker   Sherbrooke, Québec
Known as 'Ti-Père Artisse', he learned rug-making from his grandmother. He does work to pass time since an illness forced him into early retirement from his career as an electrician. He demonstrated rug-hooking for some years at the Sherbrooke Festival. Typical of the social and political commentary reflected in his art is a rug which he made in 1980 criticizing various Québec labour unions, occasioned by his having been refused medical care during a strike of medical staff.

Ref: From the Heart; National Museum of Man Archives (CCFCS)
Coll: National Museum of Man (CCFCS)

CHAPPELL, JOHN L. (1805-1878)
Woodcarver   Simcoe County
Among the waves of English settlers who came to Canada during the second
quarter of the 19th century, John L. Chappell was born in Yorkshire and emigrated to Upper Canada in 1831. He settled originally near the Sharon   49
Temple and later moved to Oro Township where he farmed throughout his
life. He is known to have been a capable woodworker, making all of his
own furniture and carving decorative motifs on axe handles. In particular he
was adept at figural carving, making various horses, deer and even a lady
rider on horse of butternut, an unusually hard wood.

Ref: Michael Rowan, 'John L. Chappell, Folk Carver'
Coll: Simcoe County Museum

CHÂTIGNY, EDMOND (1895-   )
Yard artist, woodcarver   St-Isodore, Beauce County, Québec
As a farmer, he had always managed to find occasion to carve, assemble or
create artistic works to place around the yard. When he eventually retired
and was supported by a pension, he began to devote his complete time and
energy to making owls, roosters, trees, flowers, horses, moose and other
works from wood. His creations tend to be constructed or assembled, rather
than carved. He cut out various pieces and combined them in what might
best be called 'additive sculpture'. A distinctive trademark of his work is a
field of spots which he frequently painted against a solid-colour background
on birds, flowers and other objects.

Ref: From the Heart; les patenteux du Québec
Coll: National Museum of Man (CCFCS)

CHILTON, ART (1920-   )
Decoy carver   Toronto, Ontario
A 'pupil' of the Burleigh Brothers in Toronto, Art Chilton continued their
fine carving and painting. Chilton decoys are almost reversible in that he
painted the bottoms to resemble feathers, in case the decoys should be cap-
sized. When he retired from hunting in 1969, his large rig of 250 decoys was
put up for sale, eventually to be dispersed to a wide range of dealers
and collectors.

Ref: Gates, Ontario Decoys

CINQ-MARS, CLÉMENT (1918-   )
    Woodcarver   Longueuil, Québec
A cabinetmaker by trade, he carved as a hobby throughout most of his life.
Until approximately 1960 he carved wooden figures in the round. In later

years he began to undertake relief-carving as well. His sculpture includes
many human figures, embracing couples, public officials and also some religious subjects, especially of the Virgin Mary. He has done some painting, as
well, often copying the work of other artists.

Ref: From the Heart; Waddington's catalogue (November 9-11, 1981)
Coll: National Museum of Man (CCFCS)

'CLASSICAL REVIVAL' FRAKTUR ARTIST (active 1820s and 1830s)
    Fraktur Artist   York and Waterloo Counties, Ontario
This artist, unknown by name, was in all likelihood a school teacher in the
Pennsylvania German settlement of Markham in York County. The survival
of his artistic work among descendants of his clients in both York and
Waterloo counties suggests that he was an itinerant scrivener who provided
decorated bookplates and birth records for a modest fee. His work is characterized by fine hand-lettered text and neo-classical embellishments in the
form of columns, torches, drapes and garlands.

Ref: Bird, *Ontario Fraktur;* Bird and Kobayashi, A *Splendid Harvest*
Coll: Markham District Historical Museum

CLEMENS, ABRAM S. (1790-1867)
    Fraktur artist   Waterloo County, Ontario
Abram Clemens was born in Montgomery County, Pennsylvania, and was
among a group of Mennonites who migrated northward to Upper Canada in
1825. Abram and his wife settled on a farm between Breslau and Hespeler.
He was eventually made a Mennonite minister. A small number of distinctive fraktur drawings attributed to or signed by him (one with the initials 'A
C') suggest considerable skill in this traditional Pennsylvania-German artform.
A particularly competent specimen features geometric designs, floral motifs
and winged figures, reminiscent of early motifs found on Pennsylvania fraktur and tombstones.

Ref: Bird, 'Ontario Fraktur' (the Magazine *Antiques*)
Coll: Conrad Grebel College

CLOUGH, GIBSON (1738-1799)

Sketch-artist   Louisbourg, Nova Scotia

An American with the English army of occupation after the defeat of the
French at Louisbourg, he kept a diary in which he sketched buildings and
streets of the fortress. Characteristic of the untrained artist, he uses little perspective and draws each of the walls and gates perpendicular to the sides
of the paper.

Ref: Harper, *A People's Art*
Coll: Fortress of Louisbourg National Historic Park

COATES, RICHARD (1787-1868)

Painter   Toronto, Ontario

Richard Coates distinguished himself in various artistic endeavours. Known
both as a bandmaster and painter, he was the only son of Sir Richard Coates
and Dorothy (Reynolds) Coates, a relative of Sir Joshua Reynolds. Possibly
Toronto's first resident painter, he eventually moved to the countryside
near Oakville, where he farmed. In the 1820s he did two oil paintings of a
symbolic nature for the religious group known as the Children of Peace, led
by David Willson (1778?-1866) at Sharon. These paintings were originally used
as processional banners, before later being framed and hung inside
the Temple.

Ref: Harper, *Painters and Engravers*; Harper, *A People's Art*
Coll: York County Pioneer and Historical Society, Sharon Temple

COCKAYNE, GEORGE (1906-   )

Woodcarver   Madoc, Ontario

An orphan who came to Canada in the 1920s, he led a lonely, difficult life.
Throughout his life, and especially in later years, he produced many carved
figures, often rough-hewn from posts. The great range of his work is
represented by a totem pole, many animals, relief-carved faces and figures
with grotesque elements and expressions. Most of his works are coated with
heavy applications of bright, high-gloss oil paint in contrasting or
clashing colours.

Ref: From the Heart; Inglis, *Something Out of Nothing;*
Coll: National Museum of Man (CCFCS)

CODNER, WILLIAM (active late 18th century)
    Gravestone carver   Boston, Massachusetts
A New England stonecutter, Codner's work is found also in Canada in the form of several distinctive gravemarkers (one signed) in Nova Scotia cemeteries.

Ref: Trask, *Life How Short*

CONOLLEY, HENRI (1920-   )
    Woodcarver   Pointe-Bleu Reserve, Lac-St-Jean, Québec
A Montagnais Indian, Henri Conolley does extensive whittling and carving of walking sticks and utensils, and is particularly known for the carving of heads and decorative motifs on the handles of crooked knives.

Ref: National Museum of Man Archives (CCFCS)

CONWAY, FRANK (1904-   )
    Woodcarver   Toronto, Ontario
Although he had always held a strong interest in carving, Frank Conway first made serious endeavours in the art of woodcarving upon his retirement as a Bell Telephone employee in the late 1960s. For the next several years he immersed himself in a project he had long considered – the creation of elaborate tableaux with human figures engaged in farming, domestic work and other pursuits. Using mixed hard wood and white pine, he made finely detailed depictions of persons involved in such diverse activities as spinning, shoemaking, knife sharpening, potting and blacksmithing. His most complex tableaux include a group of figures operating a printing press (modelled after a 17th-century engraving), a schoolmaster with his pupils, or musicians in a Victorian parlour. These works are boldly painted with meticulous attention given to such details as notes on music or letters on printed pages. Many of the scenes are inspired by illustrations of pioneer life in books which the carver continually consulted.

Ref: 'Carver's work is Outstanding', (*Ontario Showcase*, 1977)
Coll: Black Creek Pioneer Village

COOK, NELSON (1817-1892)
    Painter   Morrisburg area, Ontario
An itinerant painter who did oil portraits in Toronto c. 1834-37, he and his

Cook, Thomas (d. 1874). *Ella*. Oil on canvas: 1860s.

wife are listed as portrait painters in 1837. He had also done painting in New York State, and made numerous trips back to Toronto at various intervals to execute commissions.

Ref: Harper, *Painters and Engravers*; Harper, *A People's Art*
Coll: Upper Canada Village

COOK, THOMAS (-1874)

Painter   Varna, Huron County, Ontario

Thomas Cook was an entrepreneur of varied interests, having at differing times been a wagon maker, grocer, and saloon keeper in the village of Varna, near Lake Huron. He is known for a naive oil portrait of an unidentified girl seated in a simple plank chair. Although the sitter is clearly a small girl, perhaps less than ten years of age, she is depicted in typical 19th-century manner as a miniature adult.

Ref: Harper, *A People's Art*

COOK, WALTER (1923-   )

Woodcarver   Sherbrooke, Nova Scotia

This amateur artist carved a wide range of figures off and on for many years. He spent twenty-three years in the Army. After his return to civilian life he took up carving, becoming very productive in later years. His many works include birds, animals and human figures, most brightly painted.

Inf: Chris Huntington
Ref: Waddington's catalogue (June 15-17, 1980)
Coll: Art Gallery of Nova Scotia

CORRIVEAU, PIERRE (1889-   )

Yard artist   St-Gerard-des-Laurentides, St-Maurice County, Québec

He populated his yard and even the garden with deer, squirrels, cats, birds and other animals made of wood, metal and found materials. He also constructed a 'village' of birdhouses, complete with wooden or metal birds sitting, flying or feeding their young.

Ref: les patenteux du Québec

Coté, Jean-Baptiste (1834-1907). Rooster, Painted wood: late 19th century.

COTÉ, JEAN-BAPTISTE (1834-1907)

Woodcarver   Québec City, Québec

Educated at the Québec Seminary, he made a living by sculpting ships' figure-heads, cigar-store Indians and church figures. He was widely known as a wood engraver and carver. In the 1860s he created woodcuts of political caricatures. He also carved manger-scenes for various churches, and then did more elaborate furniture and mirrors. He found his chief satisfaction in the

D'Almaine, George (d. 1893). *Richard Wagstaffe, Esq.* Watercolour on paper: 1834. Coll: Niagara Historical Society.

carving of statues and relief-pictures for churches. Among religious subjects are the Nativity, Last Supper, Resurrection and others, while secular works include Louis Riel, Guttenburg and smaller subjects such as birds and animals.

Ref: Barbeau, Coté, the Woodcarver; Harper, Painters and Engravers
Coll: Fort Chambly Historical Museum; National Gallery of Canada; National Museum of Man (CCFCS); Royal Ontario Museum (Sigmund Samuel Canadian Collection)

COX, D.W. (active in 1930s)
    Woodcarver   Kings County, Nova Scotia
He did relief carving of local subjects and individuals, including a commemorative plaque for his brother Isaac Newton Cox in honour of his 90th birthday.

Ref: National Museum of Man Archives (Thomas Lackey file) (CCFCS)

CROFT, ELI (c. 1860- c. 1928)
    Woodcarver   Camperdown, Nova Scotia
A prospector and blacksmith, Eli Croft did woodworking throughout most of his active life in this Lunenburg County community. He decorated many handles of crooked knives and other utensils, as well as making and decorating shelves, coatracks, gun racks, chests of drawers and other pieces of furniture. He also carved decorative walking sticks and fashioned several large eagles.

Ref: Folk Art of Nova Scotia; From the Heart
Coll: Art Gallery of Nova Scotia; National Museum of Man (CCFCS)

CURREN, JOHN D. (1852-1940)
    Painter   Banff, Alberta
A self-taught artist, he was a prospector, miner and photographer. He was born in Scotland, and came to Alberta in 1886. He lived most of his life in Cochrane, and died in Banff. His naive images of the Banff region range from landscape views to scenes based upon memories of earlier days. His oil painting entitled 'Hot Springs, Banff, known as Cave and Basin', is a naive, yet meticulous rendering of detail, recording elements of log construction, clothing, fences and features, accompanied by explanatory inscriptions.

Ref: Edmonton Art Gallery, Painting in Alberta
Coll: Glenbow Museum

DAHLSTROM, EUGENE (1885-1971)
Painter   Hardy, Saskatchewan
A self-taught artist, he was born in Sweden and emigrated to Canada in 1912,
moving to western Canada in 1916 or 1917. He farmed in Saskatchewan, and

painted in spare time, chiefly in winter months and following his retirement. He did oil paintings of local scenes in and around the grain-elevator
town of Hardy. He worked variously with pencil drawings and oil painting
on canvas board. Typical of the subjects which he treated were 'Early Norm-
ing at Hardy', 'Homestead', 'Hardy School', and 'Sanderson's Farm'.

Ref: Harper, People's Art (catalogue)
Coll: Saskatchewan Arts Board

D'ALMAINE, GEORGE (-1893)
Painter and silhouette artist   Niagara area, Ontario
D'Almaine was born in England, and is known to have painted variously in
Baltimore, Boston, Philadelphia and New York in addition to his artistic
activity in southern Ontario. He executed numerous watercolour portraits,
miniatures and silhouettes, with several Ontario examples known from the
1830s. While in Upper Canada he painted several watercolour portraits of
leading figures in the Niagara Falls-Queenston area.

Ref: Henry and Barbara Dobson, A Provincial Elegance; Harper, A People's Art;
    Kobayashi et al., Folk Treasures of Historic Ontario
Coll: Niagara Historical Society; Toronto Public Library (John Ross
    Robertson Collection)

DALTON, SUSANNA (active 1796)
Painter   Brantford, Ontario
Daughter of Robert Prescott, Lieutenant of Lower Canada in 1796-97 and
Governor-in-Chief of Canada from 1797-1807, she is known for her water-
colour painting of Chief Joseph Brant, a work which appears to have been
modelled after the 1785 Brant portrait by English painter George Romney.

Ref: Heritage of Brant
Coll: Brantford City Hall

DARLING, JAMES (1836-1912)
Painter   Western and Central Ontario
Darling was a religious man who used artistic means to express his religious

Davies, Thomas (1737-1812). A *View of the Plundering and Burning of the City of Brymross, 1758*. Watercolour on paper: 1758. Coll: National Gallery of Canada.

commitment. Born in Scotland, he eventually became a Baptist minister. He was a self-taught artist who used painting to give visual form to biblical and moral lessons. He painted numerous cycles and panoramas between 1875-1908, including a large cyclorama housed at the Masonic Lodge in Uxbridge. He frequently used the nickname 'Nemo'.

Inf: Ed Rolph

DAUM, LEAH FREY (1896-1979)
Painter   Waterloo County, Ontario
A Mennonite woman who in her later years took up painting as a hobby, doing oil pictures which recalled her childhood recollections of life around the villages of North Woolwich and Elmira in Waterloo County. Her pictures feature public buildings and local landmarks and the fields and gardens around the home in which she was raised at North Woolwich, while others are adaptations of early lithographs and maps of Berlin, before it came to be known as Kitchener.

Inf: William and Caroline Byfield

Dawson, Richard (active mid-18th century). *View from the South-East of the Town of Placentia*. Watercolour on paper: 1758. Coll: Royal Ontario Museum.

DAVIES, THOMAS (c. 1737-1812)

Painter   Québec City, Québec

As with other topographical painters, Thomas Davies is somewhat of a marginal instance of a folk artist. He learned landscape drawing while at Royal Military Academy, Woolwich. In both Canada and the United States he executed numerous watercolour drawings of landscape features. His Canadian drawings provided early recorded views of geographical features of the Maritimes and the St. Lawrence River region.

Ref: Harper, *Painters and Engravers;* Harper, *A People's Art*
Coll: British Museum; National Gallery of Canada; New York Historical
   Society; Public Archives of Canada

DAVIDSON, FORD (active mid-20th century and after)

Woodcarver   Edmonton, Alberta

An amateur whittler and carver who made small animals and various objects for his own amusement.

Ref: Playful Objects

DAVIS, LAWRENCE (1909-1982)
Decoy and wood-carver   Toronto, Ontario
Davis was born and raised in Toronto, where he worked many years for the
T. Eaton Company. He was a carpenter by trade and was responsible for construction of floats in the annual Santa Claus Parade. In his spare time he
carved many decoys, sometimes as a family enterprise, with his wife and
daughters helping with the painting. Many of Davis' decoys were sold
through Eaton's in Toronto, as well as in stores as far-flung as New Brunswick
and Ireland. Later in life he turned also to carving other birds and animals.
His carved birds were extremely realistic, in some cases reflected in his use of
actual bird's feet on the wooden models. He kept dead birds in his freezer
from which he did studies. His first decoy was carved in 1919, while later
decoys and other birds were carved virtually up to the time of his
death in 1982.

Info: Ralph and Patricia Price
Ref: Gates, Ontario Decoys; 'Twas Ever Thus

DAWSON, RICHARD (active mid-18th century)
Painter   Newfoundland
Dawson was a captain in the British army, and for some time was in the company of cartographers sent to chart the coasts and inland waterways of
North America. While stationed at Newfoundland he produced a watercolour view of Placentia in 1758, after the British had wrested control from
the French in the conflict of 1713.

Ref: Harper, Painters and Engravers
Coll: Royal Ontario Museum (Sigmund Samuel Canadiana Collection)

DE HEER, LOUIS-CHRÉTIEN (c. 1750-c. 1808)
Painter   Montréal, Québec
Born in Guebwiller, Alsace, he migrated to Québec by c. 1787. He was an
amateur artist, working in oil, who painted numerous portraits of religious
leaders in New France. Most likely he had seen sophisticated works which
inspired his more primitive but spirited attempts.

Ref: Harper, A People's Art
Coll: Archbishop's Palace, Québec; Detroit Institute of Fine Arts; Hôtel Dieu,
     Québec; Musée du Québec

DeHeer, Louis-Chrétien (c. 1750-1808). Monseigneur Hubert. Oil on canvas: 1786. Coll: Hôpital-Générale de Québec.

DEKKERS, GEORGE (1892-   )
     Painter   North Battleford, Saskatchewan
Born at Rotterdam, Holland, he emigrated to Saskatchewan in 1912. He
worked for the Canadian National Railways from 1914 until his retirement in
1957. He began painting with the Battleford Arts Club, and is self-taught. His
subjects tend to be anecdotal, based on daily events and leisure activities, as
reflected in his oil-on-masonite picture of skaters.

Ref: Saskatchewan Arts Board
Coll: Saskatchewan Arts Board

DENNIS, EVA A. (1904-   )
     Painter   Brownlee, Saskatchewan
A number of individuals born in central or eastern Canada found their way
to the prairie provinces early in the century in search of new opportunities.
Eva Dennis was one such person, having been born at Gravenhurst, Ontario,
and moving to Moose Jaw in 1912 with her parents. She attended Teachers
College and taught in various rural schools from 1928 to 1965. She first began
to paint seriously around 1955, largely with the encouragement of her husband, Wesley C. Dennis. Drawing upon her own past experiences in the
Brownlee area, she has said, 'Instead of writing some of my memoirs, I am
trying to paint them'. Subjects treated in her varied oil paintings include
activities in the yard and classroom of Old Wives School where she had
taught many years, visiting neighbours, pioneer homesteads and local views.

Ref: Grassroots; Prairie Folk Art
Coll: National Museum of Man (CCFCS); Saskatchewan Arts Board

DENNIS, JAMES B. (1778-1885)
     Painter   Queenston, Ontario
An officer stationed with the British army in Canada during the War of
1812-14, he was an amateur painter who executed a view of the Battle of
Queenston and possibly other landscapes in the Niagara district.

Ref: Harper, Painters and Engravers; Harper, A People's Art

DENNIS, WESLEY C. (1899-   )
     Painter   Brownlee, Saskatchewan
Born at Wyoming, Ontario, the Dennis family moved west in 1900 to settle

Dennis, Eva (1904-   ). *Home Time at Capital School in Dirty Thirties.* Oil on canvas: 1960s. Coll: Saskatchewan Arts Board.

at Moose Jaw, Saskatchewan, when Wesley was only a year old. From 1925 until 1975 he farmed near Archive, and turned to painting as a hobby in the 1940s. It was especially in his retirement years that he found opportunity to paint regularly. He taught himself by imitating reproductions. Later he painted scenes which he recalled from his youth, or from earlier times in the Brownlee vicinity. In his own description of his subject matter, he called it 'nostalgia, coupled with the realization there are very few artists left who can remember the pioneer days on the prairies'. His works depict such subjects as clearing the land, storms over the valley and events in the town and surrounding countryside.

Ref: From the Heart; Grassroots; Prairie Folk Art
Coll: National Museum of Man (CCFCS); Saskatchewan Arts Board

DEPAPE, GEORGE (active 1970s)
    Yard artist   Hornby Island, British Columbia
Over a period of several years he systematically transformed the lawn of his
home into an environment of carved figures, signs, cement heads and struc-
tural forms made from wood, cement, stone, metal and found objects.

Ref: National Museum of Man Archives (Thomas Lackey file) (CCFCS)

DESCHÊNES, ALFRED (1913-1975)
    Painter   Charlevoix County, Québec
One of the group of 'Folk Painters of Charlevoix County', he is known for
various oil paintings of flowers, families in domestic settings, children in gardens and classical backgrounds, and for a picture of a father and son
strolling together.

Deschênes, Alfred (1913-1975). *Father and Son Walking (The Blind Man)*. Oil on canvas: 1930s. Coll: Dominion Gallery.

Ref: Harper, A *People's Art*; Morgan, 'Folk Painters of Charlevoix'
Coll: Dominion Gallery, Montréal

DESMAIRAIS, LOUIS (1904-   )
    Yard artist   St-Francois-du-Lac, Yamaska County, Québec   67
In the 1960s he undertook an elaborate project of constructing a grotto, or
wayside shrine, in which he utilized buttons, stones, shells, furniture parts
and other found materials.

Ref: les patenteux du Québec

DESMEULES, GEORGES (1891-   )
    Yard artist   St-Paul-de-la-Croix, Rivière-du-Loup County, Québec
Like his neighbour, Mrs. Paul Labrie, he made yard ornaments by painting
human figures on plywood, then cutting them out and placing them around
the lawn. His figures are shown in everyday working or socializing activities,
but placed in strange contexts, standing in the yard and garden. He also
carved horses and other animals, interspersed with the free-standing human
figures.

Ref: les patenteux du Québec

DEVINE, CLAYTON (1911-1981)
    Wood carver, painter   Yarmouth, Yarmouth Co., Nova Scotia
Clayton was a folk artist in the true sense, making for a period of years during his spare time as a milkman a broad range of carvings, constructions,
paintings and decoy-like ducks. Finding limited local interest in his work and
suffering from a bad back, he gave up producing his work and sold it all in
one lot about 1979. In Nova Scotia, carved oxen are often hackneyed, but
Clayton Devine's are anything but; and, for now, anyway, his reputation
rests primarily with these.

Inf: Chris Huntington

DEVINE, WILLIAM (1910-1981)
    Plaque carver   Yarmouth, Nova Scotia
William Devine, brother of Clayton Devine, was in the Canadian Armed
Forces during World War II and later worked at the Yarmouth airport. Late
in life, Devine made perhaps a dozen or so carved plaques of pine, one and

Dierlamm, Justus (1885-1971). Weathervane. Painted wood: c. 1925.

two feet long, depicting animals, fish, Adam and Eve, the evils of drink, etc. When asked why he used crayons to colour them, he answered because he used crayons as a child.

Inf: Chris Huntington

DICKIE, EVELYN (1903-   )
Quilt-maker   Meagher's Grant, Nova Scotia
Having worked in post offices in New England, as well as living in Nova Scotia, she made rich pictorial quilts drawing upon combined observation and imagination. Her unusual designs include cats and persons, and a distinctive quilt featuring a map of the village of Meagher's Grant.

Ref: Folk Art of Nova Scotia

DIERLAMM, JUSTUS (1885-1971)
Woodcarver, builder, yard artist   Neustadt, Ontario
An electrician and general handyman, he created a fantasy world in the yard around the farmhouse just north of Neustadt. Using broken glass and painted tiles, he constructed a series of mosaics set into niches in a cement and stone wall surrounding the yard. These mosaics are pictorial representa-

tions of imaginary villages and landscapes. Whimsical pierced towers at the corners and gates of the wall are partly inspired by visits he made on his motorcycle to the Canadian National Exhibition grounds and wealthy estates he passed along the lakeshore road in Oakville. In the yard are various animal sculptures made of rock and cement, as well as various weathervanes and whirligigs. In a small barn he created a 'museum' of his handiwork, until losing his eyesight in the last years of his life.

Ref: Bird and Kobayashi, A *Splendid Harvest*
Coll: Tom Thomson Art Gallery, Owen Sound

DORE, CHARLES F. (1874-1960)
     Woodcarver
A builder and contractor, he always managed to set aside time for pursuing his hobby of whittling, carving, modeling and painting.

Ref: National Museum of Man Archives (CCFCS)

DOUGLAS, VELDA
     Yard artist   Teeswater, Ontario
A life-long resident of this small community in Bruce County, she had always maintained a large garden beside her brick house. Eventually she 'augmented' the natural growth of the plot with her own varieties of flowers made of Javex bottles, plastic and metal. Many of these she painted to match real flowers, or she decorated with bright red and yellow colours, using outdoor oil paints.

Inf: Velda Douglas

DOYLE, H. (active c. 1950)
     Woodcarver   Québec
A highly capable amateur carver, he reputedly did most of his artistic work for his own enjoyment and for members of his immediate family. He is particularly known for a boldly carved male grouse or partridge, used for a nuptial procession, and signed 'H. Doyle'.

Ref: arts populaires (catalogue)
Coll: Musée du Québec

DRENTERS, YOSEF (1929-1983)
      Sculptor, painter   Rockwood, Ontario
He was born at Poppel, Belgium, and spent his early life on a farm in south
Holland. At the age of thirteen he was sent to a monastery where he spent
six years studying for the priesthood. Breaking off his classical studies, he and
the family came to Canada in 1951. He worked variously as a lumberjack,
rancher, miner and farmer, first in British Columbia and the Yukon, and later
settling on a farm near Guelph. A self-taught artist, he had a large workshop
in the former Quaker Academy at Rockwood where he lived and worked
the remainder of his life. Although he did painting and drawing, he became
best known for his sculptural works, which he took up in earnest around
1958. Many of his pieces are highly religious in nature, some having been
commissioned, and others made as an artistic statement of his own spiritual-
ity. During his lifetime he produced more than 800 pieces of sculpture, and
in 1974 he was unanimously elected a member of the Royal Canadian
Academy of Arts.

Ref: Colin S. MacDonald, A Dictionary of Canadian Artists; Kitchener-Waterloo Record
      (November 9, 1983)
Coll: Agnes Etherington Art Centre; MacDonald-Stewart Art Centre;
      Smithsonian Institution

DUHAMEL, HENRI (1909-   )
      Yard artist   St-Roch, Verchères County, Québec
Born at Ste-Théodosie, he worked at various trades, including furniture making. In the early 1960s he began his hobby of making cement lawn ornaments, notably large cactus-like plants and exotic animals, some inspired by
television programmes which he regularly watched in the evenings.

Ref: les patenteux du Québec

DULMAGE, WILLIAM Z. (1830-1913)
      Calligrapher, painter   Picton, Ontario
He is known by a pen-and-ink and watercolour drawing of a horse, done in
elaborate Spencerian decorative calligraphy. Undoubtedly derived from an
example in one of the many instruction manuals popular in the late 19th
century, this piece is distinguished by its unusually elaborate flourishes.

Ref: Harper, A People's Art

DULONGPRÉ, LOUIS (1754-1843)
    Painter   Ste-Hyacinthe, Québec
Dulongpré was an amateur painter, born at St. Denis, France. He came to
America with the French fleet in the War of Independence in 1778. He
visited Albany, then moved to Montréal, working first as a music teacher,
then an artist. He advertised in 1794 that he did portrait paintings, miniatures
and pastels. He also painted religious works as well as some still-life scenes
and landscapes.

Ref: Harper, Painters and Engravers
Coll: Detroit Institute of Fine Arts; Musée du Québec; National Gallery of
    Canada; Royal Ontario Museum (SSCC)

DULONGPRÉ, LOUIS-JOSEPH, JR. (1789-1833)
    Painter and caricaturist   Québec
Possibly a son of Louis Dulongpré, he executed various religious works,
identifiable by their peculiarly naive style, as well as portraits in the Québec
City area.

Ref: Harper, Painter and Engravers
Coll: Musée du Québec

DUPUIS, HOSANNA
    Yard artist   Maskinongé, Québec
He decorated the facade of his house with angels, crosses, a monstrance and
other religious images which he cut from plywood and painted. The yard
became a setting for a profusion of trees, birds, stars and a replica of the
Canadian Parliament Buildings in Ottawa, as well as a plywood snowmobile
in the shape of a shoe, a whimsical merging of two similar shapes.

Ref: les patenteux du Québec

E.M. (active mid-19th century)
    Theorem painter   Morrisburg area, Ontario
Known by work done in watercolour in a lady's album. He used stencils for
in-colouring in the manner of Theorem-painters.

Ref: Harper, A People's Art
Coll: Upper Canada Village

EAGLES, ELLISON (1912-1976)
    Woodcarver   North River, Lunenburg County, Nova Scotia
Working in wood camps as a saw filler, cook and blacksmith, he was able to find
free time to undertake a primitive form of carving, shaping poles with an
axe. He made human figures from stumps and created a variety of yard ornaments. During the last two years of his life he did a series of small figure groups.

Ref: Folk Art of Nova Scotia

'EARLY MARKHAM TAUFSCHEIN ARTIST' (active c. 1807-1815)
    Fraktur artist   Pennsylvania and Ontario
An itinerant scrivener and most likely also a school teacher, his work is known
in both Pennsylvania and upper York County, Ontario. Two categories of
work attributable to him include small drawings of birds and flowers presented
to pupils, and large hand-lettered and decorated birth certificates
made for families in Vaughan and Markham Townships of York County.

Ref: Bird, Ontario Fraktur; Bird and Kobayashi, A Splendid Harvest
Coll: Markham District Historical Museum; National Museum of Man (CCFCS)

EBERHARDT, NICHOLAS (active 1863-1879)
    Potter   Toronto, Ontario
Born in France, he produced a wide variety of utilitarian stonewares after his
arrival in Canada. He decorated many of his pieces with distinctive cobalt-
blue floral designs.

Ref: Newlands, Early Ontario Potters; Webster, Early Canadian Pottery
Coll: Royal Ontario Museum (Sigmund Samuel Canadiana Collection)

EBERSOL, BARBARA (1846-1922)
    Fraktur artist   Lancaster County, Pennsylvania
A member of the Amish community of eastern Pennsylvania, this self-taught
artist inscribed and decorated many bookplates, using fraktur lettering and
floral motifs. The existence of several examples among the Amish Mennonites of Waterloo and Perth counties in Ontario raises the question of
whether Barbara Ebersol may have visited Canada at some time, or whether
Ontario Amish may have made occasional trips into Pennsylvania.

Coll: Amish Historical Library, Aylmer

Eisenhauer, Collins (1898-   ). *Adam and Eve*. Painted wood: c. 1970. Coll:
National Museum of Man (CCFCS).

EBY, WILLIAM (1831-1910)
Potter   York and Waterloo counties, Ontario
A village potter who made earthenware storage and kitchen pieces for the
Mennonite communities of Markham Township in York County and
Woolwich Township in Waterloo County. At least one piece made at Mark-
ham features Pennsylvania-German folk art designs as glaze decoration, while
at the Conestogo Pottery in Waterloo County he produced specialty pieces

and miniatures for his family with distinctive decorative embellishments.

Ref: Newlands, *Early Ontario Potters;* Webster, *Early Canadian Pottery;* Webster, *The William Eby Pottery*

74

Coll: Doon Pioneer Village and Heritage Museum; Joseph Schneider Haus Museum; Markham District Historical Museum; National Museum of Man (History); Royal Ontario Museum (Sigmund Samuel Canadiana Collection)

EISENHAUER, COLLINS (1898-   )
   Woodcarver   Union Square, Lunenburg County, Nova Scotia
As a youth he quit school at age 13 to help the family, doing odd jobs –
apple picking, logging, working on Ontario tobacco farms, and even boat
work on journeys to Barbados. In early life he did some graphic work –
painting and drawing postcards. His carving career was inaugurated in 1964
with the making of a swan, followed by carvings of cats, human figures,
lovers, a policeman, Adam and Eve and even Colonel Saunders. His group
settings often convey humour, sexual fantasy and irony.

Ref: *Folk Art of Nova Scotia; From the Heart*
Coll: Art Gallery of Nova Scotia; National Museum of Man (CCFCS)

ELDER, EDWARD C. (active late 19th and early 20th century)
   Painter   Hampton, New Brunswick
He was one of four brothers who painted and decorated buildings in and
around Hampton. Particularly well-known is his oil picture, *An Edwardian
Table*, painted in 1903.

Ref: Harper, *A People's Art*
Coll: New Brunswick Museum

ELLIOT, JOHN (c. 1885-1971)
   Woodcarver, boat builder   Coburg, Ontario
Emigrating from England in the early 1900s, he worked on the prairies at
various jobs. He had always wished to be an artist and began to carve upon
his return to Ontario. He made boat models well into the 1960s, as well as
models of farm implements, threshers, tractors and other vehicles.

Ref: National Museum of Man Archives (Thomas Lackey file) (CCFCS)

ELLIS, WILLIAM (1870s-1960)
    Decoy carver   Whitby, Ontario
After selling his apple orchard in the 1920s, Billy Ellis suddenly found himself
having much more time than previously to devote to hunting, fishing and
making decoys. He had a shack on Story's Marsh south of Whitby where he   75
carved decoys, selling them through a local sports store. He produced a
unique style in his low head decoys.

Ref: Gates, *Ontario Decoys; 'Twas Ever Thus*

ENNS, CORNELIUS (1884-1960)
    Clock maker   Edenburg, Saskatchewan
A retired farmer and handyman, he repaired clocks, being completely self-
taught. In the 1950s he made a clock, adapted from the traditional 'Kroeger'
hanging clock found in areas of German settlement. He used many found
objects, including even parts of pitchforks and other implements, and he
painted or used decals for decoration on the clock face.

Ref: Bird and Kobayashi, A *Splendid Harvest*

ERWIN, ARTHUR (active 1970s)
    Woodcarver   Winchester, Ontario
He took up carving in 1969, a few years before his retirement. His first carvings were of small animals. He later made a totem pole and life-size human
figures, many constructed from laminated pine boards which he carved with
saw and chisel.

Ref: National Museum of Man Archives (CCFCS)

EVERTON, NATHANIEL BIRD (active 1930s and after)
    Woodcarver, collage artist   Toronto, Ontario
Raised on a farm in the Forest Hill Village area of present-day Toronto, he
had various jobs – delivering milk, a greaser at the roundhouse, lumbering,
cartage-work and fire-fighting. Late in life he pursued woodcarving and
assemblage as a hobby. Among his works are carved Indians, cowboys, RCMP
figures, dancers, fire-fighters and other pieces.

Ref: Mazelow Gallery, Toronto.

FANCY, LARRY (1951-   )
    Woodcarver   Milton, Queens Co., Nova Scotia
Following his father's interest in carving, Larry began making similar pieces
in 1980. Among these are foot-high lumberjacks, smaller birds, larger hawks
with open wings, a few television personalities, etc.

Inf: Chris Huntington
Ref: Waddington's catalogue (June 15-17, 1980)

new

FANCY, RAYMOND (1910-   )
    Woodcarver   Milton, Queens County, Nova Scotia
Ray Fancy might be called a disciple of the Ralph Boutilier school (see entry).
Ray lives in a trailer across the road from Ralph and has admired Ralph's
genius first-hand for years. In about 1976, Ray had become curious enough to
see what he could produce. Fighting a very serious heart condition, he tried
some of Ralph's motifs and he has always felt fairly humble about his results.
Because of his health problems, Ray has not produced a lot of work. Though
he has a humble attitude about his work, it is all his own and commands its
own attention. During his working years he worked at the lumber trade and
as a carpenter.

Inf: Chris Huntington

FARRAR, EBENEZER (active c. 1840-1857)
    Potter   St. Johns, Québec
Founder, along with his brother Moses, of the earliest stoneware pottery in
Canada, c. 1840. The Farrars also operated a pottery at Fairfax, Vermont.
Several pieces bear distinctive blue-decorated design-work characteristic of
this craftsman.

Ref: Webster, *Early Canadian Pottery*
Coll: Royal Ontario Museum (Sigmund Samuel Canadiana Collection)

FARRAR, GEORGE W. (active 1857-1890)
    Potter   St. Johns and Iberville, Québec
He took over the stoneware pottery at St. Johns upon the death of his
father in 1857. After a fire in 1876 he moved the pottery to Iberville. The
firm in later years made Rockingham-type and imitation-Wedgewood wares,
but for many years was known for blue-decorated stoneware.

Ref: Webster, *Early Canadian Pottery*
Coll: Royal Ontario Museum (Sigmund Samuel Canadiana Collection)

FARRAR, MOSES (active c. 1840-c. 1850s)
    Potter   St. Johns, Québec
Founded the stoneware pottery (with his brother Ebenezer) at St. Johns c.
1840. Producer of blue-decorated wares.

Ref: Webster, *Early Canadian Pottery*

FERNLUND, IVAR GUSTAV (1881-1933)
    Decoy carver   Hamilton, Ontario
Fernlund migrated from the United States, settling at Hamilton in 1906.
Always a meticulous craftsman, he began making decoys in 1912 from observation of actual birds. His hollow decoys are finely carved and painted with
artist's oils.

Ref: Gates, *Ontario Decoys*

FILLION, VALÈRE (1892-   )
    Table and gamesboard maker   Senneterre, Abitibi County, Québec
He made many elaborate gamestables and boards, inlaying small pieces
together to form intricate decorative patterns. Additionally, he carved walking sticks with geometric designs and animal or human faces.

Ref: les patenteux du Québec

FINLAY, GEORGE E. (1918-   )
    Sketch-artist   Fort Garry, Manitoba
A topographical artist, he was sent to Fort Garry in the Red River District in
1846 as a result of tensions with the United states over the Oregon District.
While there (1846-48) he executed a series of pen drawings, including several
Indian figure studies.

Ref: Harper, *Painter and Engravers*
Coll: Fort Garry Museum

FLACK, DAVID A. (active 1869-1970)
    Potter   Picton, Ontario

In partnership with Isaac Van Arsdale, he succeeded Oren Ballard in the production of blue-decorated stoneware at Cornwall, Ontario, using a stylized bird-motif. He had been a potter in New York State prior to coming to Canada in 1869.

Ref: Newlands, *Early Ontario Potters*; Webster, *Early Canadian Pottery*
Coll: Royal Ontario Museum (Sigmund Samuel Canadian Collection)

FLANCER, LUDWIG (1902-1980)
    Painter   Montréal, Québec

A versatile painter of landscapes, city scenes, interiors, still-life compositions, portraits, animals, biblical and symbolic subjects. Much of his work is a celebration of divine creation, using the Montréal and Québec countryside as subject matter. Like Arthur Villeneuve, he was a barber-turned-artist. His cityscapes suggest a melancholic view of a world in which nature is increasingly subjugated to the encroachment of urban development. His nature-pictures reveal a vital, radiant presence in trees and flowers. Other subjects reflect his Jewish upbringing, or are observations of details of everyday domestic life.

Ref: Home Again gallery catalogue (Sept. / Oct. 1981)
Coll: Montréal Museum of Fine Arts

FLETCHER, ED (1900-   )
    Painter   Melfort, Saskatchewan

A self-taught artist, he began painting regularly in his 60s, following a heart attack. He acknowledged that his doctor had gotten him started with drawing and painting as a form of therapeutic activity. He did various subjects in watercolour, notably landscapes, animals and some local scenes.

Ref: Grassroots; National Museum of Man Archives (Thomas Lackey file) (CCFCS)

FLETCHER, ERNIE (active 1970s and after)
    Yard artist   Chatham, Ontario

Maker of whirligigs, weathervanes and varied wooden lawn ornaments. Many of his pieces are inspired by cartoon and comic-book characters, made of cut and painted plywood.

Inf: Ernie Fletcher

FLETT, ARTHUR L. (1900-   )
    Woodcarver, builder   Winnipeg, Manitoba
He produced a great many woodcarvings in the form of animals, human
figures and miniature buildings such as log cabins, outhouses and other structures. Some of his decorative work is combined with functional considera-
tions, notably in the form of lamps with stagecoaches and horses integral to
the structure of the lighting device.

Ref: Folk Art in Canada (catalogue); From the Heart
Coll: National Museum of Man (CCFCS)

FORREST, CHARLES REMUS (active 1821-23)
    Painter, sketch-artist   Québec
An aide-de-camp for the Earl of Dalhousie (1770-1828), Forrest came to Canada
on an inspection tour. He did watercolour views on this journey, showing
scenes on the French River at points along the way in Québec.

Ref: Harper, Painters and Engravers; Harper, A People's Art
Coll: National Gallery of Canada; Royal Ontario Museum (Sigmund Samuel
    Canadiana Collection)

FOSTER, SUMNER
    Woodcarver   Port George, Annapolis Co., Nova Scotia
Sumner Foster is now an elderly man who is no longer producing. He made
numerous carvings of animals, deer heads with antlers and other subjects.

Inf: Chris Huntington
Coll: Art Gallery of Nova Scotia

FOTHERGILL, CHARLES (1782-1840)
    Painter   Rice Lake, Ontario
A printer and publisher, as well as a leading naturalist, Fothergill was a pro-
moter of the arts after arriving in Canada from his home in Yorkshire, England. He proposed the Lyceum of Fine Arts for Toronto in 1835. While it is
stretching a point to consider Fothergill a folk artist, some of his watercolour
landscapes of Rice Lake and Port Hope reveal a naive quality. His notebooks
are of particular historical importance with their detailed ornithological and
natural history studies.

Ref: Harper, *Painters and Engravers*; Harper, *A People's Art*
Coll: Royal Ontario Museum (Sigmund Samuel Canadiana Collection and
    Zoology); University of Toronto Library

80   FOX, MANASSE
    Woodcarver, furniture maker   Nain, Labrador, Newfoundland
A self-taught woodworker, Manasse Fox is particularly known for a unique
handmade cupboard on which he carved and painted a complex array of
geometric elements c. 1900. The designs and colours appear to be of Inuit
derivation, resembling closely the decoration on traditional skin boots.

Ref: Walter Peddle, *The Traditional Furniture of Outport Newfoundland*

FREY, CHRISTLE NORMAN (1886-c. 1950)
    Painter   Ontario, Alberta and British Columbia
Born at Morriston in Wellington County, Ontario, C.N. Frey moved to Calgary in 1908. He advertised himself as 'General Illustrator and Topographical
Real Estate Artist'. He later lived in British Columbia and had exhibitions of
his work in North Vancouver. He did many oil paintings of landscapes,
pioneer settlements, historical and anecdotal events having to do with
discovery and settlement of western Canada.

Ref: *From the Heart*; Harper, *A People's Art*
Coll: National Museum of Man (CCFCS); National Gallery of Canada

FRANCIS, MARY (1900-1979)
    Painter   Picton, Ontario
Mary Francis was a self-taught artist who took up painting as a hobby around
1950. Her sources appear to be a combination of observation and imagination. In the former category are pictures of household pets or garden
flowers, while the latter includes compostions of animals placed against con-
trived backgrounds. Using left-over house paints, she rendered charming
depictions of horses, dogs and other animals on sheets of masonite.

Inf: Ralph and Patricia Price
Coll: National Museum of Man (CCFCS)

GAGNON, CHARLES (active 1970s and after)
Woodcarver   Joussard, Alberta
In retirement he took up a hobby of whittling and carving, and is known as
the maker of various toys, animals and whimsical carved objects.

Ref: Playful Objects

GALL, JOHN (active 1940s and after)
Woodcarver and builder   Saskatchewan
His sculptures are of varied materials, including wood, concrete, metal and
other elements. Some of his works are based on news events, notably a concrete castwork entitled 'Moon Landing' (1970), while others are drawn from
natural observation or based upon anecdotes, including subjects such as
'Wedding', 'Accident', 'Stump-Pulling', as well as a miniature store, a motor-
ized mill and other buildings.

Ref: National Museum of Man Archives (Thomas Lackey file) (CCFCS)

GALLANT, ART (-1980)
Woodcarver   Dieppe, New Brunswick
Carving in the round or in relief, Art Gallant has derived many of his themes
from mass media, current events and popular culture. His various tableaux
tend to be highly expressive in mood, frequently satirical or lightly
humorous. He has carved political caricatures and tongue-in-cheek interpretations of film and media characters, as well as unusual anecdotes suggested
in group carvings.

Ref: 'Twas Ever Thus; Waddington's catalogue
Coll: National Museum of Man (CCFCS)

GARCEAU, ALFRED (1888-   )
Woodcarver   Grand-Mère, Laviolette County, Québec
He worked at many odd jobs, including that of water-carrier, supplying the
boilers of boats in the region. He began carving at the age of 65, using a
knife to carve soft wood. His first works included totems and various
human figures.

Ref: les patenteux du Québec

Geisel, Albert (1889-1973). Flowers. Painted metal: c. 1950.

GEISEL, ALBERT (1889-1973)

Yard artist   Elmira, Ontario

He was a prodigious maker of yard ornaments, whirligigs, floral arrangements, clocks, weathervanes and other objects from found materials in
wood, metal, glass and plastic. He decorated the lawn of his house on Queen
Street in Elmira, as well as the interior, including sponge-painted designs
on the floors.

Ref: Kobayashi et al, *Folk Treasures of Ontario; Primitive and Folk Art*
   (UW catalogue)

Gemeinhardt, John (1826-1912). Carousel horse. Painted wood:
late 19th century.

GÉLINAS, FLORIDA (1900-   )

Yard artist   St-Matthieu, St-Maurice County, Québec

Late in life she undertook a project of constructing a miniature village,
comprised of plywood houses, stores and churches, using her lawn
as a 'landscape'.

Ref: les patenteux du Québec

GEMEINHARDT, JOHN (1826-1912)

Woodcarver, cabinetmaker   Bayfield, Huron County, Ontario

An immigrant cabinetmaker from Germany, he settled at Bayfield in the
early 1850s, where he was engaged in a wide range of activities, among them

furniture making, carpentry, decoy-carving, cooperage and undertaking. In the 1880s and 1890s he made several specialty pieces of furniture and decorative accessories for members of his own family, and especially upon the occasion of the marriages of each of his four daughters. In his drawingbooks are sketches of furniture and architectural elements, as well as poetry of his own creation.

Ref: Bird, *Perpetuation and Adaptation: The Life and Work of John Gemeinhardt*; Bird and Kobayashi, A *Splendid Harvest*

GILLEN, MARGARET (GERVIN) (active c. 1860s and 1870s)
    Painter   Brantford, Ontario
This amateur painter did several oil portraits for family members and other persons in the Brantford area. She received awards for her portraits and crayon drawings. In 1864 she did paintings on wooden panels which she exhibited at the Upper Canada Provincial Exhibition.

Ref: Harper, *Painters and Engravers*; *Heritage of Brant*

GIROUX, ALBERT (1892-   )
    Yard artist   Ste-Anne-de-la-Pérade, Champlain County, Québec
A tailor by trade, he used his free time to carve and construct plaques and free-standing figures. Some of his themes are inspired by earlier travels in Europe, the Near East and the United States. Working in both wood and marble, he sculpted human figures, faces in low-relief, a plaque recording his marriage in 1919, a family coat of arms, tribute-plaques for Canada and for Québec and each of the provinces. He also made model churches, houses and a tall inlaid case to support a station-master's clock.

Ref: *les patenteux du Québec*

GISSING, ROLAND (1895-1967)
    Painter   Alberta
A nephew of the English critic George Gissing, he emigrated to Canada in 1913 at the age of eighteen. He worked as a cowboy, and later became a rancher. Largely self-taught, he had only a few years of art training in Edinburgh before emigrating. By 1934 he was a full-time painter. His pink sunsets with purple clouds over blue mountains above yellow fields give a distinctive charm to his landscapes.

Ref: *Painting in Alberta*
Coll: Glenbow Museum

GLASS, SAMUEL (active 1886-late 1890s)
　　Potter　　　　　　　　　　　　Tillsonburg and London, Ontario　　85
He was a maker of blue-decorated stoneware, at first in partnership with
William Gray of Tillsonburg, then with his brother John H. Glass at London.

Ref: Newlands, *Early Ontario Potters*

GOOLD, FRANKLIN P. (active 1859-1867)
　　Potter　　　　　　　　　　　　　　　Brantford, Ontario
Whether as an actual technician or a good manager, Goold's period as opera-
tor of the Brantford Pottery saw the greatest range of decorative treatment
of wares, dramatically embellished with flowers, birds, cows, horses and
other motifs, sometimes incised as well as painted.

Ref: Newlands, *Early Ontario Potters*; Webster, *Early Canadian Pottery*
Coll: Royal Ontario Museum (Sigmund Samuel Canadiana Collection)

GOYER, JOHN (active 1960s and after)
　　Woodcarver　　　　　　　　　　　　　　Ottawa
A highly competent carver, he has done elaborate works both as free-
standing subjects and as relief-carved tableaux.

Ref: National Museum of Man Archives (CCFCS)

GRAHAM, JOHN (active 1827-1880)
　　Woodcarver　　　　　　　　　Saint John, New Brunswick
An exceptionally skillful carver, he is reputedly the artist who sculpted
several outstanding ship's figure-heads in the mid-19th century, and possibly
the carver of plaques, trade signs and cigar-store Indians.

Ref: Harper, *People's Art* (catalogue)
Coll: New Brunswick Museum

GRAVEL, A. (active late 19th century)
　　Painter　　　　　　　　　　　　　　　Québec
He is known for a watercolour painting of a Montréal house,

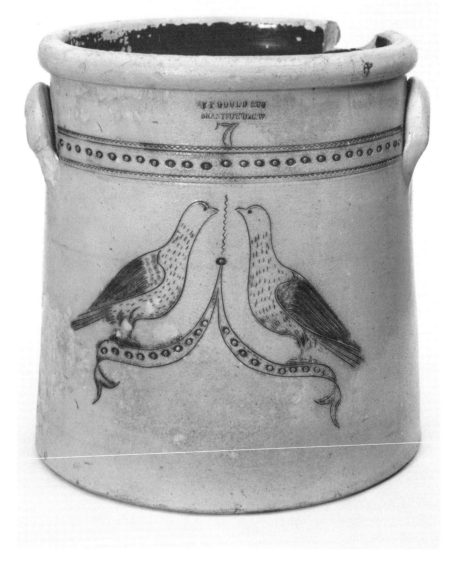

Goold, Franklin P. (active 1859-1867). Decorated storage jar. Glazed
stoneware: 1860s. Coll: Royal Ontario Museum.

reflecting competent drafting ability and simplicity of composition.

Ref: Harper, *A People's Art*

GRAY, WILLIAM JR. (active 1883-1886)
　　Potter　　　　　　　　　　　　　　　　Tillsonburg, Ontario
Gray was a maker of blue-decorated stoneware, as well as later Rockingham
wares. He worked in partnership with Spence H. Betts at the
Tillsonburg Pottery.

Ref: Newlands, *Early Ontario Potters*

GREG, RADA (1941-　　)
　　Painter　　　　　　　　　　　　　　　　Toronto, Ontario
Born in Yugoslavia, she came to Canada in 1975. She is self-taught, and has
painted full-time since 1978. She documents Toronto's ever-changing neigh-
bourhoods, and provides bird's-eye views of major streets in the city. Her
colours are exceptionally bright, and buildings tilt away from each other to
permit maximum insertion of trees, people, and other details. She exhibited
her work at the Toronto Primitives show in January / February, 1984. Among
her favourite subjects are livingroom interiors, gardens, orchards and festive
street scenes. She works in oil, and develops compositions and colour
schemes reminiscent of many European naive painters.

Ref: Toronto Primitives
Coll: National Museum of Man (CCFCS)

GRENIER, ALPHONSE (1908-　　)
　　Yard artist, woodcarver　　St-Jean-de-la-Lande, Beauce County, Québec
After raising 18 children, he found left-over time to undertake his hobby of
woodcarving, and began to assemble weathervanes, whirligigs and birds, the
latter with wind-powered tails. His whirligigs are comprised of musicians,
dancers, acrobats and persons engaged in farming, woodcutting or other
tasks. His outstanding project is a large music box with many moving dancers, musicians and other figures involved in activities both ordinary
and extraordinary.

Ref: les patenteux du Québec; From the Heart
Coll: National Museum of Man (CCFCS)

Graham, John (active 1827-1880). Indian hunter. Painted wood: c. 1830. Coll: New Brunswick Museum.

GUY, CLOVIS-EDOUARD (1819-1910)
Woodcarver   Québec
He carved and painted numerous religious subjects, including the Last
Supper, and various bas-relief tableaux.

Ref: arts populaires catalogue
Coll: Musée du Québec

H.B. (active c. 1885)
Painter   Montréal, Québec
This artist is known for a signed oil painting of a social gathering at the
Charles Lumkin half-way house north of Mount Royal. Possibly derived from
a lithograph, this painting is charming in its bright colours.

Ref: Harper, People's Art (catalogue)
Coll: McCord Museum

HALE, ELIZABETH (1774-1826)
Painter   York (Toronto), Ontario
A topographical artist, and the wife of John Hale, she is said to have come to
Canada as early as 1793. She executed watercolour views of her husband's
seignory at Ste-Anne-de-la-Pérade, and of Québec, Sherbrooke and Montréal
districts, and of York (Toronto), c. 1803-04. She was principally a painter of
landscapes, but also of habitants and Indians.

Ref: Harper, Painters and Engravers; Harper, A People's Art
Coll: W.H. Coverdale Collection, Manoir Richelieu, Québec;
      Public Archives of Canada

HALE, WILLIAM (active 1840s)
Painter   Kingston, Ontario
Among his oil portraits are one of Mrs. Robert Smith, reported to be
Canada's first woman doctor, painted at Kingston. He was probably an
itinerant portrait painter. Known examples are rendered in primitive style,
with hard outlines, lack of modelling, and a tendency toward embellishment
by innumerable small details.

Ref: Harper, Painters and Engravers; Harper, A People's Art
Coll: Winnipeg Art Gallery

Harbuz, Ann Alexandra (1908-   ). Portrait of Ukrainian Girl. Acrylic on canvas: 1970s. Coll: National Museum of Man (CCFCS).

HALFYARD, JOHN (1880-1974)
    Doll-maker   Alberni Valley, British Columbia
Born in Jersey in the Channel Islands, John and his brother survived difficult
circumstances, having been deserted by alcoholic parents. He never learned
to read or write more than his own signature. Migrating to Canada in his
30s, he reached Kapuskasing in northern Ontario, then worked his way west-
ward across the country, labouring on farms, railroads and circuses. At age
85, with hearing and sight failing, he began to make dolls from found materials. His subjects include birds, animals, human figures, scarecrows, circus performers, dancers, even a self-portrait. In 1974 his dolls were selected for exhibition in the 'In Praise of Hands' show initiated by the Ontario Science
Centre in Toronto.

Ref: National Museum of Man Archives (CCFCS); *Westworld* (September /
    October 1976)

HANSEN, FRANCES (1918-   )
    Painter   Spruce Home, Alberta
Born at Prince Albert, Saskatchewan, she attended Teachers College in Saskatoon. She had some lessons at Murray Point Art School, and at the Emma
Lake Artists Workshop with A. Kenderdine and George Swinton. A part-
time teacher, she is largely self-taught, painting landscapes and anecdotal subject matter, generally as watercolour works.

Ref: Saskatchewan Arts Board
Coll: Saskatchewan Arts Board

HARBUZ, ANN ALEXANDRA (1908-   )
    Painter   North Battleford, Saskatchewan
Ann Harbuz was born in Winnipeg, Manitoba, of Ukranian descent, and
spent most of her childhood years in Whitkow, Saskatchewan. She later
lived in the Richard and Hafford areas of Saskatchewan. Her painting career
seems to have been initiated in 1967, after seeing a neighbour's (Mike
Poryvizniak) efforts. She works in both acrylic and oil, and her pictures frequently recall her homeland and early Canadian childhood. She painted
many landscapes and subjects based on stories of pioneer life. Her pictures
generally relate happy remembrances (in contrast to the more 'down to the
ground' works of Molly Lenhardt). Her first works were of still-life subjects
and of Easter eggs. Her later work is more complex, with elaborate over-

painting and perspective. Among subjects treated are local farms and home-steads, village business establishments, scenes from everyday pioneer life, dances and ritual activities.

Ref: From the Heart; Grassroots Saskatchewan catalogue; *Prairie Folk Art*
Coll: National Museum of Man (CCFCS); Saskatchewan Arts Board

HARD, GEORGE (1850-1935)
Woodcarver   Toronto and Markdale, Ontario
Born in England, he moved to Canada at a young age. He was a crane opera-tor for the Canadian National Railroad in Toronto, retiring in 1915 at age 65. He moved to Markdale in Grey County where he took up carving for a pas-time. He is particularly known for a carved whimsy, a 'Good Book' contain-ing a viper which springs out to sting the hand of the unsuspecting person opening the cover.

Ref: From the Heart; National Museum of Man Archives (CCFCS)
Coll: National Museum of Man (CCFCS)

HARNESS, LAURA (1928-   )
Painter   Arborfield,Saskatchewan
This amateur artist began sketching early in her life. She also carved figures of horses from plaster of Paris in the 1950s, and began to paint in oils in 1965. Her pictures are frequently anecdotal and highly nostalgic, portraying happy moments, amusing incidents or sad times. She was inspired in part by the wildlife paintings of artist Clarence Tillenus. Representative titles of her works include 'Monarch', 'Wild and Free', 'Feeding the Cows', 'Abandoned Car', 'The Day Disaster Struck', and 'The Old Livestock Loader'.

Ref: Grassroots Saskatchewan catalogue; *Seven Saskatchewan Folk Artists*
Coll: Saskatchewan Arts Board

HART, WILLIAM (active 1849-1855)
Potter   Picton, Ontario
Hart was a member of a prominent family at Ogdensburg, New York, com-ing to Canada in 1849, where he established a stoneware pottery at Picton. He sold the pottery in 1855, returning to New York and working there until his death in 1869. Hart pottery is distinguished by its blue-decorative treat-ment, featuring flowers, bees and other designs.

Ref: Newlands, *Early Ontario Potters*
Coll: Royal Ontario Museum (Sigmund Samuel Canadiana Collection)

HAY, JAMES (active c. 1775-1795)
Gravestone carver   Halifax, Nova Scotia
Among the earliest of identified stone cutters of Nova Scotia, and the carver
of a 1776 stone with winged head, rosettes and floral border. The Hay
workshop involved also a son, John Hay. Among stones possibly carved in
this shop are several in Halifax, New Glasgow and Lunenburg, and an
unusual 'Adam-and-Eve' tombstone at Saint Paul's Burial Ground in Halifax.

Ref: Trask, *Life How Short*
Coll: Nova Scotia Museum

HENDERSON, SIR EDMUND YEAMANS WOLCOTT (1821-1896)
Painter   Kingston, Ontario
Henderson was an engineer and topographer with the Royal Engineers in
the British army, and was stationed in Canada 1839-1845 and 1847-48. While
serving on the boundary commission he did a report with panoramic
sketches of the country, and is particularly known for a scene of himself and
a fellow-officer making a social call in Kingston. He was a highly skilled
draftsman and watercolour painter, whose work occasionally suggests a simplicity akin to that of self-taught artists.

Ref: Harper, *Painters and Engravers*; Harper, *A People's Art*

HENDERSON, NICKOLAS (1862-1934)
Painter   Kingston, Ontario
Born at Jones Falls, Ontario, he studied variously at Royal Military College,
Kingston, and in Chicago. He made numerous sea voyages, and later in life
operated a coal business in Portsmouth (Kingston). He had studied painting
with Forshaw Day while at Royal Military College (Day's only Canadian
pupil). He painted until 1932, exhibiting both watercolour and oil paintings
of ships and landscapes.

Ref: Harper, *Painters and Engravers*

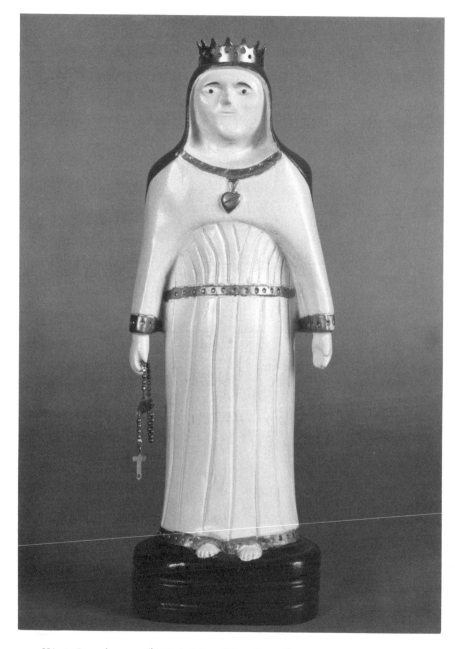

Héon, Oscar (1901-1976). *Virgin Mary*. Painted wood: c. 1950.
Coll: Québec Museum.

HÉON, OSCAR (1901-1976)
    Woodcarver   Cap-de-la-Madeleine, Québec
Héon was an amateur whittler and carver who made many religious figures,
toys, dioramas, tableaux, sometimes drawing upon events from everyday
life, other times from happenings reported in the media. His secular figures
exhibit considerable humour, in the manner of caricatures, while his religious works are charming in their simplicity, echoing the quiet humility of
fellow carver Philippe Roy.

Ref: arts populaires catalogue; *From the Heart;* '*Twas Ever Thus*
Coll: Musée du Québec; National Museum of Man (CCFCS)

HERRON, ART (1880-1960s)
    Decoy carver   Peterborough, Ontario
Art Herron hunted extensively at Kawartha Lakes during the early part of
the century. Although he carved many decoys on request for local hunters,
he also was kept busy meeting a steady demand through an agent in Chicago. Herron decoys tend to have smooth finishes, and some are highly
colourful with mottled paint treatment.

Ref: Gates, *Ontario Decoys*

HEWITSON, MRS. A. (active 1930s)
    Sculptor   Toronto, Ontario
Working in crepe paper and cardboard, Mrs. Hewitson and Mrs. I. Woodall
constructed a miniature orchestra comprised of conductor, instrumentalists
and vocalists. This elaborate work was exhibited at the Women's Building of
the Canadian National Exhibition, and won first prize for the years 1933-37.

Ref: Waddington's catalogue (November 9-11, 1981)

HIBBARD, CLEM (1905-   )
    Yard artist   Lancaster, Ontario
The Hibbard family lived for many years at Pointe Claire, Québec. He later
worked at many odd jobs, including a tree nursery in Detroit. Clem settled
at Lancaster in 1966, and began immediately to transform his large yard into
one of Canada's most colourful sculptural 'environments'. He had on earlier
occasion constructed doll houses and toys for his children, but not until the
move to Lancaster, strategically fronting onto Highway 401, did he com-

Hoover, Christian L. (1835-1918). Fraktur birth-and-baptismal record.
Watercolour on paper: 1854.

mence upon the ambitious project of making special displays for Christmas,
Halloween and Valentine's Day, and an ongoing proliferation of trees,
flowers, animals, human figures and other works made from plywood, metal
and found objects. Some of the pieces are accompanied by humorous
inscriptions, and many are wry commentary upon contemporary news
events. When asked about motivation, Clem answered that he loved to see
the reaction of neighbours and the many travelers whom he managed to
lure off the expressway for a closer look.

Inf: Clem Hibbard

HILTZ, ORRAN (1901-1978)

Decoy carver — Lunenburg County, Nova Scotia

A fisherman at Indian Point on Nova Scotia's South Shore, Orran Hiltz was a sufficiently capable decoy maker that others copied his patterns. His work is recognizable by its dramatic stylization, as in his Mergansers with upswept tails, large head profiles and relief-carved wings.

Ref: Kangas and Kangas, *Decoys: A North American Survey*

HOFFMAN, FRED G. (1845-1926)

Woodcarver — Waterloo and Oxford counties, Ontario

Hoffman was a transient who reputedly came to Canada from Pennsylvania under questionable circumstances at the turn of the century. He lived for varying periods of time in the homes of Mennonites in Waterloo County in the summers and Amish in Oxford County in the winters. In gratitude for the hospitality of his hosts, he made pencil drawings and carved elaborate shelves, wallboxes and other articles, decorated with carved and painted stars, geometric motifs and other designs. Most bear pencil inscriptions in his florid hand, dedicating these tokens of appreciation to various Mennonite and Amish recipients.

Ref: Kobayashi, 'Fred G. Hoffman (1845-1926)'

HOOVER, CHRISTIAN L. (1835-1918)

Fraktur artist — Markham Township, York County, Ontario

Born near the village of Markham, he is perhaps unique in having become a fraktur artist almost against his own wishes. He took up the pastime of making hand-lettered and decorated birth records for family and friends as a means to while away idle time when serious illness forced his quarantine and long period of recuperation in 1854-55. Upon his return to good health, he appears to have abandoned his artistic pursuit. In later years he became deacon of the Wideman Mennonite Church north of Markham.

Ref: Bird, *Ontario Fraktur*; Bird and Kobayashi, A *Splendid Harvest*
Coll: Markham District Historical Museum

HOPKINS, ELISABETH (1895-   )

Painter — Sturdies Bay, British Columbia

Her career was launched at the mature age of 81, when she placed a small

Horst, David B. (1873-1965). Animals. Painted wood: c. 1935-43.

painting in an arts and crafts show on Galiano Island where she lived. It was priced at $5 and purchased by John Korner, a well-known Vancouver artist. Later, Xisa Huang, director of a Vancouver art gallery visited Elizabeth and bought the whole lot. Her watercolour pictures of trees, bushes, flowers and grasses, inhabited by ducks wearing kerchiefs or cats playing ring-around-the-rosie, are child-like not only in their subject matter but in their naive manner of execution.

Ref: *Cambridge Daily Reporter* (Galt, Ontario: January 19, 1984)

HORST, DAVID B. (1873-1965)
   Woodcarver   Waterloo County, Ontario
As a youth, he had been involved in numerous unsuccessful business adventures, having travelled to Michigan and Florida in search of opportunity. He returned to the Mennonite community of Saint Jacobs, Ontario, where he held various odd jobs. Late in life, following two tragic events – the death of his wife and his own serious stroke in 1935 – he took up carving and painting of domestic animals, most given as presents to children and as tokens of gratitude to friends and members of the community who looked after him. Competent carving and colourful stipple-painted decoration give his carvings a unique charm.

Ref: Kobayashi, 'Folk Art in Wood: David B. Horst'; Bird and Kobayashi, A
  Splendid Harvest
Coll: National Museum of Man (CCFCS)

'HORTON CARVER' (active c. 1783-1793)
    Gravestone carver   Kings County, Nova Scotia
One of the earliest of indigenous Nova Scotia tombstone carvers, this craftsman frequently left his 'trademark' in the form of a tree-and-axe motif cut
into the gravemarker. His work is to be found on numerous stones in Kings
and Colchester counties.

Ref: Trask, Life How Short

HORWOOD, H. (active c. 1867-1890s)
    Glass painter   Prescott, Ontario
He established a coloured glass business in Prescott in 1876, painting
memorial windows and supplying geometrical designs in crayon or colour.
He exhibited a specimen in 1890 with portraits of Canadian political leaders.
Some of his paintings reveal a primitive quality, as in the pictures of livestock, gardens and other subjects which he painted on windows of the house
of J.M. Wiser, a distiller in Prescott.

Ref: Harper, Painters and Engravers; Harper, A People's Art
Coll: Upper Canada Village

HOTO, ALBERT (active 1940s and after)
    Woodcarver   Stromness, Ontario
Working at various odd jobs, this talented craftsman made his own sign
advertising himself as a sign painter and ornamental carver. Working in a
small shed near Lake Erie in Welland County, he carved numerous small
animals, both domestic and exotic, with considerable refinement of detail
and attractive painted finishes.

Ref: Kobayashi et al, Folk Treasures of Historic Ontario; 'Twas Ever Thus

HOWARD, SIDNEY (1913-   )
    Woodcarver   Sidney and Albert Bridge, Cape Breton, Nova Scotia
Around many odd tasks and carpentry work he managed to find opportunity for pursuit of his wood carving interests, particularly after 1945. His earli-

Hoto, Albert (active 1940s and after). Owl. Painted wood: c. 1950.

est carving, a deer, was inspired by a drawing in his daughter's colouring book. He continued to carve cats, fish, birds and human figures. Many of his works were destroyed in a fire in the late 1960s. He eventually began to undertake the ambitious project of carving life-size figures, including his interpretation of Cape Breton's legendary 'McAskill Giant'. He also carved various low-relief plaques with nature-scenes, such as a beaver in a marsh setting, or scenes with stags, horses, seals, fish and sailing vessels. Inspired also by popular culture, he carved large sharks modelled after the villain in the movie *Jaws*. He also carved political figures and an RCMP officer. By the 1980s he was turning increasingly to television programmes for subject matter.

Ref: Folk Art of Nova Scotia; Waddington's catalogue (June 21-22, 1982)

HUGHES, MRS. JAMES (active 1880s)
    Rug maker   Blockhouse, Nova Scotia
She is known on the basis of an extraordinary designed and hooked rug, dated 1888 and featuring her signature in the border.

Ref: Decorated Nova Scotia Furnishings

HUDSON, THOMAS (1886-   )
    Painter   Pouch Cove, Newfoundland
A life-long resident of this village near St. John's, he did not take up painting until he was 85 years old. His subjects were frequently taken from calendar illustrations, other times from memory. Working in tempera on cardboard, he depicted familiar stores, houses and topographical landmarks in the Pouch Cove area.

Ref: Memorial University Art Gallery catalogue, Folk Images '77

HUMBERSTONE, SIMON THOMAS (active c. 1860-1902)
    Potter   Toronto, Ontario
Succeeding his grandfather and father in the stoneware business, he made blue-decorated pottery at Newton Brook, near Yonge Street and Steeles Avenue in present-day metro Toronto. In the 1890s, responding to public taste, he made unglazed wares that could be painted, a favourite pastime of the period.

Ref: Newlands, *Early Ontario Potters*

Hunsicker, Isaac Z. (1803-1870). Fraktur birth-and-baptismal record.
Watercolour on paper: 1836. Coll: Philadelphia Free Library.

HUMMEL, JOHN (1892-1970)
    Woodcarver   Maryhill, Ontario
A farmer in this German community in Waterloo County, he began woodcarving following an accident involving a fall from a roof which left him partially paralyzed in the 1960s. He initially carved animals and birds for his own
amusement, then made several pieces for a parade in commemoration of
the Canadian Centennial in 1967. He carved several elaborate bird-trees in
the last years of his life.

Ref: Bird and Kobayashi, A *Splendid Harvest*
Coll: Doon Pioneer Village and Heritage Museum; Joseph Schneider Haus
    Museum; National Museum of Man (CCFCS)

HUNSICKER, ISAAC Z. (1803-1870)
    Fraktur artist   Berlin (Kitchener), Ontario
Hunsicker was a Pennsylvania school teacher who migrated to Canada
between 1832-35. He lived near Breslau and Berlin (present-day Kitchener) in
Waterloo County, where he produced refined fraktur specimens, initially in
the form of drawings of birds and flowers for pupils. Throughout much of
his life he continued to produce bookplates, birth records and family registers in his superb calligraphic hand for the Mennonite community.

Ref: Bird, *Ontario Fraktur*; Bird and Kobayashi, A *Splendid Harvest*
Coll: Doon Pioneer Village and Heritage Museum; National Museum of Man
    (CCFCS)

HUTCHINS, SAM (1894-   )
    Decoy carver   Jones Falls, Ontario
Working variously as a trapper, trucker and farmer, he carved many decoys
early in his life, and then at late age. He initially made drawings of birds,
some of which served as models for his carving. He often made decoys from
cedar fence posts, using pine for the heads. Many of his finer examples
feature elaborate gouch-carving or cross-hatching, an aesthetic touch which
was probably motivated by the functional need of reducing glare when wet.
Most of his decoys were sold to hunters north of Gananoque and along the
Rideau Canal System.

Ref: Gates, *Ontario Decoy; From the Heart*
Coll: National Museum of Man (CCFCS)

INCE, CAPTAIN (active 1758)
Painter   Louisbourg, Nova Scotia
Stationed with the British army at Louisbourg during the siege of 1758, he is
believed to be the artist who did a portrait of General Wolfe during the
battle, signed 'Capt. Inch' (Ince?). The work is stylistically related to a hand-
ful of other works of the period.

Ref: Canadian Magazine (Toronto: June 18, 1918, p. 130); Harper, *Painters and
Engravers*
Coll: Royal Ontario Museum (Sigmund Samuel Canadiana Collection)

'J.W. CARVER' (active c. 1820-1839)
Gravestone carver   Hants, County, Nova Scotia
Using slate from the quarry at Gore, this carver inscribed the initials 'J.W.'
on several tombstones. Distinctive carved motifs include hands, coffin shapes
and geometric designs.

Ref: Trask, *Life How Short*

JACOBI, DANIEL (active 1874-1905)
Potter   Waterloo, Ontario
A maker of utilitarian earthenwares for the local Germanic community, he
also is known for unique whimseys and specialty pieces made for his own
family, including numerous miniatures and a hand-assembled reclining dog.
He experimented with many glaze effects, using colours of green, brown
and others achieved by addition of metallic oxides during firing.

Ref: Bird and Kobayashi, A *Splendid Harvest*; Newlands, *Early Ontario Potters*
Coll: Royal Ontario Museum (Sigmund Samuel Canadiana Collection)

JAMESON, ANNA BROWNELL (MURPHY) (1794-1860)
Painter   Great Lakes region
An amateur painter and critic, daughter of Brownell Murphy, Irish miniature
painter. She was married to Robert S. Jameson in 1822, later following him to
Canada upon his appointment as Attorney-General of Upper Canada in 1836.
She spent 15 months in Canada, and did sketches of travels around the Great
Lakes area. She retired to Kensal Green, England. Many of her sketches were
undertaken to illustrate her writings.

Jasmin, Edouard (1905-   ). *La boucherie*, 1900. Glazed earthenware: c. 1976-77.

Ref: Harper, *Painters and Engravers*
Coll: British Museum; Ontario Archives; Royal Ontario Museum (Sigmund
    Samuel Canadiana Collection)

JAMIESON, JAMES (active 1960s and after)
    Woodcarver, painter   Six Nations Reserve, Middleport, Ontario
A carver of birds and animals, often on wood plaques. Some depict geese in
flight, a moose crossing a river, or other scenes observed or imagined from
nature. He is also known to have carved a bust portrait of
a cigar-store Indian.

Ref: Waddington's catalogue (October 6-7, 1981)

JASMIN, EDOUARD (1905-   )
    Ceramicist   Montréal, Québec
Edouard Jasmin is an unusual figure in that he is the only known Canadian

Jobin, Louis (1845-1928). *The Jolly Tar*. Painted wood: c. 1870. Coll: Château de Ramezay.

folk-artist to produce pictorial work in clay. In his earlier years he painted
and drew sketches of religious and local subjects. By the 1950s he began to
create painted murals, using a mixture of sand, pigment, glue and water.
Most of the early works are based upon biblical scenes or upon events from
his personal past. In the late 1960s his interests were broadened by the
accidental discovery of clay when a neighbour's basement was being exca-
vated. Without benefit of any formal artistic training, Jasmin experimented
with in-the-round sculptures, relief plaques and ceramic bottles. The bottles
enclose biblical and personal worlds of experience, viewed through 'windows' cut out on several sides. The wall plaques frequently depict religious
occasions, such as the celebration of Mass, or daily incidents, such as an argu-
ment in a traffic jam. Many are comprised of scenes set in stores, streets,
schools, churches or at home, while a recurring theme is that of the humour
underlying the business of living from day to day. In many cases, lettered
texts serve as narrative commentary to the tableaux worked in relief.

Ref: Louis J. Gioia, 'Edouard Jasmin'; Gloria Lesser and Leopold L. Foulem,
   'Edouard Jasmin: Folk Ceramicist'

JEDDRY, CLARENCE (active 1940s and after)
   Woodcarver   Clyde River, Shelburne Co., Nova Scotia
Clarence Jeddry in later years was to become a refined woodworker. Beginning in the late 1940s he made a small number of painted carvings of
cowboys on bucking horses, a bearded fiddler, an old woman knitting in a
rocker, a Dutch girl with flowers, and other subjects.

Inf: Chris Huntington

JOBIN, LOUIS (1845-1928)
   Woodcarver   Ste-Anne-de-Beaupré, Québec
His style was affected strongly by the Gothic Revival of the mid-19th century, yet his art retained much of a personal folk art quality. He considered
himself more of an artisan than an artist. He carved an enormous range of
works both secular and religious. Late in life he was fully preoccupied with
the carving of animals, angels, saints and madonnas in his tiny workshop at
Ste-Anne-de-Beaupré.

Ref: Harper, *People's Art* (catalogue)
Coll: Art Gallery of Ontario; Musée du Québec; National Gallery of Canada

JOE, MENDELSON (1944-   )
    Painter   Toronto, Ontario
Born in Toronto, he received a B.A. at the University of Toronto. He began
painting in 1975 after several years of clothing and jewellery design. He is an
accomplished musician who writes and records his own songs. He exhibited
in the Toronto Primitives show at Market Gallery in January / February 1984,
with oil paintings of life in the city, flying, driving and other aspects of urban
living. His association with professional artists and awareness of technique
may suggest that he stands somewhat on the boundary between folk and
academic art.

Ref: *Toronto Primitives*

JOHNSTON, GEORGE (active 1970s and after)
    Woodcarver   Renfrew County, Ontario
This retired construction worker first began to involve himself with carving
as a hobby in the late 1970s. He carves full-size birds, singly or in group settings, using acrylics over a base coat of gesso on basswood, pine or beech
wood. His birds are frequently depicted in familiar settings – standing, hover-
ing, feeding, perched on branches or stumps. He also has carved various
animals of the forest, and has received awards at the Canadian National
Exhibition.

Ref: Waddington's catalogue (June 21-22, 1982)

JOLY, ERNEST (1904-   )
    Yard artist   Chomedey, Fabre County, Québec
He initially constructed bird-houses, but after a visit to Cap-de-la-Madeleine,
where he saw the work of others (possibly Oscar Héon), he turned to making varied carved works, including elaborate boat-weathervanes and
horse-whirligigs.

Ref: *les patenteux du Québec*

JONES, ELIZABETH (1805-1890)
    Painter   Brantford, Ontario
Born in England, she was the wife of Peter Jones, the Indian Wesleyan minister. She is known for several watercolour works attributed to her, one of
which is believed to have been inspired by an illustrated collection of Long-

fellow poetry and ballads (*Hiawatha's Wedding*). Exhibiting in the 1854 Upper Canada Provincial Exhibition, she received awards for her miniature watercolour paintings.

Ref: Heritage of Brant; Harper, *Painters and Engravers*

JOST, EDWARD R. (active 1864)
    Cabinetmaker, painter   Halifax, Nova Scotia
As suggested by his painting *Ulysses*, and was possibly inspired by illustrations from such popular sources as the widely-read *Age of Fables* by Thomas Bullfinch. His painted adaptation, a colourful oil work, reveals a certain naivete in composition and colour.

Ref: Harper, *Painters and Engravers*; Harper, *A People's Art*

JUBE, HERBERT (active mid-20th century and after)
    Painter   Iroquois, Ontario
Herbert Jube appears to be an interesting example of painters who utilize their artistic abilities to give visual expression of their memories. An illustration of this type of painting is his 1957 rendering in oil, entitled 'Scenes of Our School Days', with its charming images of boats, a large Canada Steamship Lines vessel and cars travelling along the Saint Lawrence River past the village of Iroquois.

Ref: 'Twas Ever Thus

KENYON, J.J. (1862-1937)
    Painter   Oxford and Waterloo counties, Ontario
Kenyon was born at Washington, in Oxford County, then lived variously at nearby Berlin and Blair. What little instruction he may have received in art was received in Berlin, where he eventually became a photographer. He was a keen lover of horses, owning several of his own and regularly travelling to the 'Great Circuit' races in New York and Kentucky. It is reported that he earned some income by selling his horse portraits to owners of winning animals. He also made photographs of animals at small fairs and at the Royal Winter Fair in Toronto. Many of his paintings were undoubtedly made from such photographs, with backgrounds and titles added at the artist's or owner's discretion.

Kenyon, J.J. (1862-1937). *Sunbeam*. Oil on panel: c. 1870. Coll:
Royal Ontario Museum.

Ref: Harper, *People's Art* (catalogue); Kobayashi, 'Local Paintings Tour Canada'
Coll: Royal Ontario Museum (Sigmund Samuel Canadiana Collection)

KIMBALL, CHESTER N. (active late 18th century)
   Gravestone carver   London, Connecticut
Chester Kimball was a New England stonecutter whose work is known in
Canada by gravestones in several Nova Scotia cemeteries.

Ref: Trask, *Life How Short*

KLEMPP, JOHN P. (1857-1914)
   Cabinetmaker   Neustadt, Ontario
Following in the footsteps of his father, John P. Klempp was a carpenter and
cabinetmaker who maintained a furniture-making workshop as well as a
hotel business in Neustadt and, later, Walkerton. He worked in a strongly

Germanic decorative tradition, doing elaborate inlay work on the surfaces of hardwood wardrobes, cupboards and other pieces made in the 1870s and 1880s. His repertoire of traditional folk art motifs included tulips, birds, hearts, paired horses, trees and geometric designs.

Ref: Bird, 'Furniture as Folk Art; John P. Klempp'; Bird and Kobayashi, A
    Splendid Harvest
Coll: Bruce County Museum; National Museum of Man (History Division)

KNAZE, MIRO T. (active 1950s and after)
    Woodcarver   Keswick, Ontario
Carving primarily in low relief, his subjects include both religious and secular themes, among them being a mother and child, an Indian portrait, and miniature carved replicas of churches and other buildings.

Ref: National Museum of Man Archives (CCFCS)

new) KNOCKTON, JOHN (1901-1980)
    Wood carver   Bolyston, Guysborough Co., Nova Scotia
This folk artist was handy at carving things for placement around the house during his early married life and before. He worked as a lumberjack, on the roads of Guysborough and as a farmer and fisherman. Knockton made a broad range of eccentric sculptures, most with simple mechanics, and often used neon paints. He carved canes and made birds out of gnarls found in the woods around his farm.

Inf: Chris Huntington

KOCEVAR, FRANK (1899-1982)
    Painter   Kelowna, British Columbia
Kocevar was an immigrant from Slovenia, Yugoslavia, who had worked in his youth in the family vineyard and was employed eleven years as the church bell-ringer. After emigrating to Canada, he worked variously as a farm hand and a miner. He had originally rented land, and was to have his farming career virtually terminated when drought and a grasshopper plague destroyed his crop in 1936. After retirement from work in the Kimberley Mines in 1964 he turned to painting for a hobby, intensified by a visit to Expo '67 in Montréal, where he confessed to preferring the Old Masters to most of the contemporary painting on display. He painted continuously during the last

Klempp, John P. (1857-1914). Inlaid wardrobe. Mixed hardwoods: c. 1875.
Coll: National Museum of Man (History Division).

Kocevar, Frank (1889-1982). *Worried Mother*: Oil on hardboard: 1964-1979. Coll: National Museum of Man (CCFCS).

fifteen years of his life, doing oils based upon memories of early life in Slovenia and Canada. His subjects cover a wide range of moods, from the bitter reality of war to the sustaining warmth of domestic life.

Ref: Folk Art in Canada (catalogue); *From the Heart*
Coll: National Museum of Man (CCFCS)

KOSTIUK, LENA (active 1970s and after)
    Painter   Saskatchewan
An amateur painter who depicted scenes from pioneer life, emphasizing such subjects as planting time, domestic chores, house-building, arrival at the homestead and special family occasions.

Ref: National Museum of Man Archives (Thomas Lackey file) (CCFCS)

KUEPFER, DANIEL (active 1950s)
    Woodcarver   Millbank, Perth County, Ontario
This retired farmer in the Old Order Amish settlement of Perth County
whittled and carved various animals for his immediate family, as well as distinctive small birds mounted on heart-shaped bases.

Ref: Bird and Kobayashi, A *Splendid Harvest*

KUPESIC, RAJKA (1952-   )
    Painter   Toronto, Ontario
Born in Yugoslavia, she came to Canada in 1978. She had initially pursued a
career in dance and was a member of the National Ballet of Zagreb. She
lived briefly in Munich, where she was affiliated with the School of Naive
Painters. She exhibited in the Toronto Primitives show in January / February
1984. In contrast to the large, bird's-eye views of Toronto rendered by Rada
Gregg, her focus is more intimately directed toward the activities of Kensington Market, of fans standing in front of Old Massey Hall or the new Roy
Thomson Hall, or of musicians, marchers or celebrants at special civic events.
As a professional, she should not be considered so much a 'folk' artist as
rather an academically sophisticated artist who has chosen themes of naive
art as her subject matter.

Ref: Toronto Primitives
Coll: Toronto Symphony Orchestra

KURELEK, WILLIAM (1927-1977)
    Painter   Alberta, Manitoba and Toronto, Ontario
William Kurelek grew up in Alberta and Manitoba, born of Ukrainian
parents who had joined the earlier migrations in search of new economic
and religious opportunity in Western Canada. This cultural heritage figured
prominently in paintings of aspects of his own background and in his sym-
pathetic treatment in art of other religious and ethnic traditions. William
attended the University of Manitoba and studied art briefly in Toronto and
Mexico. In other respects he was largely self-taught painter. Working in an
economical or linear style, he produced paintings of his youth, scenes of Polish or Jewish life, or biblical stories, as well as many other subjects which possess a fresh and childlike appearance. He is also important for having given
serious attention to the artistic significance of picture frames, many of which
he carved or painted in a manner derived from Ukrainian traditional
decorative arts.

Ref: Kurelek, Someone With Me
Coll: Art Gallery of Hamilton; National Gallery of Canada; National Museum of Man (CCFCS), Others

KUZELA, MIROSLAV (active late 1960s and early 1970s)
    Painter   Toronto, Ontario
An immigrant who came to Canada in 1967, he did a number of oil paintings of familiar urban and residential sections of Toronto. Bright colours and geometric elements in his paintings may have been inspired by traditional decorative arts of his Czechoslovakian homeland, to which he later returned.

Ref: Harper, *A People's Art*

LABBÉ, JOSEPH (active 1970s and after)
new
    Yard artist, woodcarver   Belle River, Essex County, Ontario
The Labbé family moved to this French-speaking district of western Ontario, leaving Québec when Joseph was nine years old and not yet able to speak a word of English. A self-taught cabinetmaker, he makes cupboards, book shelves and other pieces, as well as many smaller objects, including bird houses, doll houses and miniature furniture. He has also made several crucifixes with inlaid symbolic details. In 1982 he constructed a large working windmill for the yard, and on the occasion of the annual fiddlers' contest at Belle River he made an extraordinary violin more than twelve feet in length.

Inf: Joseph Labbé

LABRIE, MRS. PAUL (1921-   )
    Yard artist   St.Paul-de-la-Croix, Riviere-du-Loup County, Québec
She painted many scenes on plywood, and, in many cases, cut out the human figures, depicting various activities of weaving, knitting, carrying maple sugar, playing table games or other domestic pursuits.

Ref: les patenteux du Québec

LABROSSE, ONÉSIME (active early 20th century)
    Woodcarver   Montebello, Québec
A 'walker' for a lumber company, he marked trees for cutting while his wife and 13 children tended the farm at Montebello. He is known for a remark-

Labrosse, Onésime (active early 20th century). Love-seat. Painted wood: 1909.

able carved love-seat which he constructed and decorated for his wife in 1909. Its carved device of clasped hands was reputedly intended to symbolize the strength of the marriage bond despite long and frequent separations.

Ref: From the Heart

LACOMBE, PAUL EMILE (1914-   )
    Decoy carver   Louiseville, Québec
A prolific craftsman, Paul Lacombe made a wide range of birds for a period of more than a half-century. His most typical decoys are geese, mergansers and wood ducks. Many are finished with homemade metal tools, used to stamp an image of feathers and wings. Among his finest decoys are examples which he has painted with meticulous detail.

Ref: Kangas and Kangas, *Decoys: A North American Survey*

Laithwaite, George (1873-1956). *George and His Friends.* Sculptured cement:
c. 1915-30.

LACZKO, WILLIAM (1927-   )
   Woodcarver   St. Brieux, Saskatchewan
Having worked variously at farming and mining, he did not undertake his
hobby of woodcarving until 1978, after lightened farm responsibilities coupled with having seen the work of another craftsman (Wilf Neill) at Fort
Smith provided inspiration. Using the wood from birch trees cut down to
make room for a recreation-room addition to his house, he carved an owl
for his wife on her birthday. Subsequently he carved geese, fish and even
human figures. Much of his initial work was done for family and friends, but
eventually he began to offer pieces for sale and exhibited work in local art
and craft shows.

Ref: National Museum of Man Archives (CCFCS); *Prince Albert Daily Herald*
   (February 24, 1982)

LAITHWAITE, GEORGE (1873-1956)
   Sculptor   Goderich, Ontario
George Laithwaite established himself as a farmer at the east edge of this
Huron County community, then worked actively between 1915 and 1956
creating many sculptural works in cement, stone, metal and found materials,
including even gravemarkers. He emphasized human figures, many as a form
of satirical or political commentary, frequently in response to world-events.
Other figures and groupings are based upon radio or comic-strip characters.
By 1945 he had begun to receive so many visitors that he erected a stone
coach house which served as his studio, and in which he installed a pipe
organ which he played on Sunday afternoons.

Ref: *Grassroots Art; Primitives and Folk Art* (UW catalogue)

LAJOIE, JOSEPH (1894-   )
   Yard artist, woodcarver St-Gabriel-de-Brandon, Berthier County, Québec
After his retirement from farming, Joseph moved into town where he lived
in a rented house. In the yard he carved or constructed countless whirligigs,
some with horses and human figures, and made numerous clusters of birds
perched on 'trees' made from actual branches.

Ref: *les patenteux du Québec*

Lajoie, Joseph (1894-   ). Bird-tree. Painted wood: 1970s.

LAKE, ANGUS (active 1920s and 1930s)
Decoy carver   Westlake, Ontario
The postmaster of the village of West Lake for several years, he was a
prolific carver of decoys. To lighten his birds he drilled as many as a dozen
wide holes in the bottom and filled them with cork.

Ref: Gates, *Ontario Decoys*; National Museum of Man Archives (CCFCS)

LANGILLE, DAVID M. (active 1950s and after)
Woodcarver   Halifax County, Nova Scotia
David Langille began to pursue carving as a pastime in his later years. He
carved numerous farm animals, implements and human figures engaged in
various forms of agrarian activity.

Ref: National Museum of Man Archives (CCFCS)

LAPEER, LYNDA (1949-   )
Painter   Port Hope, Ontario
She began painting in the winter of 1977, when paralyzed with Guilliane-
Barré Syndrome. Her first subjects are her doctors looking down upon her.
Many of her works, done in acrylic on canvas, are interior details, domestic
subjects or the outdoor world of the picturesque Northumberland Hills.

Ref: Good Heavens (catalogue)

LATSCHAW, ABRAHAM (1799-1870)
Fraktur artist   Waterloo County, Ontario
Latschaw was an immigrant craftsman from Berks County, Pennsylvania, who
emigrated to Waterloo County in 1822. In his first years he proved himself a
master fraktur artist, producing the rich illuminated pages of the bible of
Bishop Benjamin Eby. He was also a cabinetmaker at Manheim and New
Hamburg, and several pieces from his workshop feature inlaid tulips, painted
compass stars, trees and other folk art motifs.

Ref: Bird, *Ontario Fraktur*; Bird and Kobayashi, A *Splendid Harvest*; Bird, 'From
    Calligraphy to Cabinetmaking: Abraham Latschaw'
Coll: Joseph Schneider Haus; Kitchener Public Library and Waterloo Historical
    Society; National Museum of Man (History Division); Philadelphia
    Free Library

Latschaw, Abraham (1799-1870). Fraktur bookplate and genealogy.
Watercolour on paper: February 19, 1823.

LAVOIE, PAUL-HENRI (1920-   )

Yard artist   St-Nazaire, Lac-St-Jean County, Québec

He would often 'find' sculptural forms in the forest in unusual fungi or
branches resembling animals or other subjects. He placed these around his
yard amidst flowers, fences, bridges or totem poles which he made of wood.
In winter he sculpted snow figures of caribou, seals and human characters.

Ref: les patenteux du Québec

LAW, GORDON (1914-   )

Woodcarver   Near Oshawa, Ontario

He began carving when his father died in 1979. Having helped his father in
the latter's carving projects, Gordon did not take up the hobby fully until
later, recalling that his father 'thought it would be nice if I carried on but he
didn't think it would be good if I started while he was still doing it'. When

Law, Gordon (1914-   ). Figures from Classical Mythology.
Painted wood: c. 1980.

still in his teens Gordon began to write poetry. His fascination with Greek
and Roman mythology is reflected in several of his carvings, including a
series of Greek and Roman deities. In 1980 he published a booklet of his
poems along with pictures of carvings on such subjects as Theseus and the
Minotaur, Pandora's Box, Oedipus and the Sphinx and other mythological
themes. He had been foreman in charge of repairs at General Motors for 25
years. In later years he made a circus, Noah's ark, a carousel and
Mennonite buggies.

Inf: Gordon Law
Ref: *Good Heavens* (catalogue); Gordon Law, *Mythy Poems*

LAW, IVAN (c. 1885-1979)
    Woodcarver, model builder   Oshawa, Ontario
He took up his carving hobby at age 79, after retirement from the hardship
of farming. He claimed to have been inspired by a trip along the St.
Lawrence River past Québec City, where he saw a moose carved by a
French-Canadian craftsman. He began carving that winter, making buffalo,
horses and pigs, as well as miniature houses and churches. His son Gordon
estimated that Ivan carved over 600 pieces, including human figures, horse-
and-wagon teams, animal groupings and scenes of domestic work,
blacksmithing and milking cows.

Ref: Ivan Law Carvings (catalogue); *'Twas Ever Thus*
Coll: National Museum of Man (CCFCS)

LAZIER, GEORGE I. (active 1864-1887)
Potter   Picton, Ontario   123
He succeeded Samuel Skinner at the pottery in Picton, producing blue-
decorated stoneware for two decades, the last several years in partnership
with three other entrepreneurs. Designs used by Lazier included flowers,
birds and distinctive homely or humorous mottoes inscribed in blue, as in an
example with the words, 'Look Here'.

Ref: Newlands, *Early Ontario Potters*; Webster, *Early Canadian Pottery*
Coll: Royal Ontario Museum (Sigmund Samuel Canadiana Collection)

LE BER, PIERRE (1669-1707)
Painter   Montréal, Québec
Pierre Le Ber was among the earliest of Canadian nativeborn artists. In 1694
he joined the religious community of the Charon Brothers, otherwise
known as the Hospitalers of Joseph of the Cross. Le Ber taught painting in
the first arts and crafts school in Montréal from 1694 to 1706, just before his
death, after which the project was discontinued. In 1697 he designed the
chapel of St. Anne, decorating it with his own paintings. Le Ber is especially
remembered for an extraordinarily simple but expressive oil painting of
Marguerite Bourgeoys, foundress of the Congregation of Nôtre-Dame. Much
has been said concerning her aversion to the vanity of a portrait, even a
painting which would eventually be commissioned as a posthumous
memorial to this spiritual leader. The portrait is rendered in the stylized *orans*
style, befitting the piety of the nun, yet is also highly expressive in its portrayal of a serenely sad countenance. Its starkness may be argued in part
because of its function as a funeral portrait, but, at the same time, it suggests
certain technical limitations of an artist uncertain as to means of properly
rendering texture and sculptural volume.

Ref: Harper, *Painting in Canada*; Lord, *The History of Canadian Art*
Coll: Sisters of the Congregation of Nôtre-Dame

LEBOEUF, OREL (1886-1968)
Decoy carver   St. Anicet, Québec
Perhaps one of the recognized 'masters' of decoy carving, Orel Leboeuf pur-

LeBer, Pierre (1669-1707). *Marguerite Bourgeoys*. Oil on canvas: 1700. Coll: Sisters of the Congregation of Notre-Dame.

LeBouef, Orel (1886-1968). Decoy. Painted wood: early 20th century.

sued his craft for almost seventy years. His work might well be compared with the finest of late 19th century carving for which Québec is famous. He made many varieties of floating ducks, and also a rare standing example, all distinguished by meticulous carved detail, and beautifully incised feathers on wings and tail. In addition, his various bluebills, black ducks and canvasback drakes feature unusually skillful painted treatment. His career came to an abrupt end in 1965 when his cabin-workshop was destroyed by fire.

Ref: Kangas and Kangas, *Decoys: A North American Survey*

LÉGARÉ, JOSEPH (1795-1855)
    Painter   Québec City, Québec
Considered to be Canada's first landscape painter, and perhaps earliest historical painter as well, the range and quantity of Légaré's artistic productivity was truly monumental. Most of his work reveals a sophistication which can

Légaré, Joseph (1795-1855). *Cholera Plague, Québec*. Oil on canvas: 1837. Coll: National Gallery of Canada.

hardly permit him to be categorized as a folk artist, the case being feasible perhaps on the basis of a few of his local views. Notable among these are the relatively primitive pictures of 'The Falls at Saint-Ferréol', or 'The Artist's House at Gentilly, P.Q..' Given the technical refinement of his historical, landscape and religious paintings, as well as his competent copies of European works from the Desjardins collection, the best that might be said on this point is that he was a thoroughly accomplished academic artist, though self-taught, and that on rare occasion he produced some works of a less rigorous quality than his usually formal work. It would be difficult to deal with the ultimately ironic suggestion that Québec's most academic of portrait painters, Antoine Plamondon, who studied under Légaré, had actually learned his craft from a folk artist!

Ref: Harper, *Painting in Canada*; Macdonald, A *Dictionary of Canadian Artists*
Coll: Laval University; Musée du Québec; National Gallery of Canada;
   Montréal Museum of Fine Arts

LENHARDT, MOLLY (1920-   )
    Painter   Melville, Saskatchewan
She was born in the Winnipegosis area, Manitoba. Self-taught, she was
encouraged in painting by her father when she was a child. After the family
moved to Melville, Saskatchewan, she continued to paint in oil, depicting   127
many aspects of memories of her childhood, of the years of early settlement
in Saskatchewan, and of stories told of her Ukrainian background. Frequently her pictures testify to the hardships of impoverished peasant life.
Working in a dimly-lit alcove at the back of her confectionery store or in
her kitchen-studio at home, she painted many scenes emphasizing local
places of interest, family events, portraits of her parents, pioneer days,
Ukrainian dancers and others in traditional costume and fantasy-themes.

Ref: From the Heart; Grassroots Saskatchewan (catalogue); Prairie Folk Art; Seven
    Saskatchewan Folk Artists
Coll: National Museum of Man (CCFCS); Saskatchewan Arts Board

LENT, BENJAMIN (active late 1820s and 1830s)
    Potter   Lincoln County, Ontario
Lent was an immigrant from New Jersey who produced decorated
earthenware in both the United States and Canada. He used incised decoration and painted designs, imitating sgraffito techniques used earlier by German potters in the United States. Known Lent pottery is distinguished by
tulips and other traditional Pennsylvania-German folk art motifs.

Ref: Newlands, Early Ontario Potters; Rupp, 'The B. Lent Pottery'
Coll: Brock University; Henry Ford Museum and Dearborn Village; Jordan
    Museum of The Twenty

LESSARD, EMILE (1909-   )
    Yard artist, painter, woodcarver   Maskinongé, Québec
A retired farmer and church custodian, he painted throughout most of his
life, sometimes imitating Old Masters or early Canadian paintings illustrated
in books. His later paintings emphasize current and historical scenes in the
immediate vicinity of Maskinongé, as well as domestic and family events. He
also carved numerous life-size animals in his back yard, and spent many years
constructing a miniature (ratio 1:12) version of the church and presbytery,
fitted with miniature furnishings which he carved or assembled from wood.

Lenhardt, Molly (1920-   ). *Ballet Dancer, Ukrainian National Festival*. Oil on canvas: c. 1976. Coll: National Museum of Man (CCFCS).

Lessard, Emile (1909-   ). *Québec Farmstead*. Oil on canvas: c. 1975.

Inf: Emile Lessard
Ref: Bird, *Canadian Folk Art*

LEVY, LINDSEY (1892-1980)
Decoy carver   Little Tancook Island, Nova Scotia
In contrast to the carvings of many of his Nova Scotia contemporaries, the
decoys made by Lindsey Levy are wide and stubby in appearance, and lack
the carved wings characteristic of makers such as Fred Nickerson of Villagedale. Instead, his ducks have smooth surfaces, even to the point of having no
eyes, and features are suggested less by carving than by painting.

Ref: Kangas and Kangas, *Decoys: A North American Survey*

LEWIS, EVERETT (1893-1980)
Painter   Marshalltown, Digby County, Nova Scotia
Growing up as a farm labourer and fish peddler, he married Maud Dowlet

Lewis, Maud (1903-1970). *Two Oxen: Winter.* Oil on board: c. 1950.

and became night watchman at the Marshalltown Poor Farm. Later, retired, he took up painting maritime scenes, landscapes with animals and other subjects in acrylic. He was largely overshadowed by the more widely-known work of his wife, Maud Lewis. He was murdered in 1980 by a would-be robber.

Ref: Folk Art of Nova Scotia
Coll: Art Gallery of Nova Scotia; National Museum of Man (CCFCS)

LEWIS, MAUD (1903-1970)
   Painter   Marshalltown, Digby County, Nova Scotia
She was born in the village of Ohio in Yarmouth County, enduring considerable hardship in her early life. She was severely deformed and partially crippled from polio, and experienced the death of both parents in her youth. She married Everett Lewis in 1921 and attempted to help overcome their

poverty by selling fish. She also made hand-drawn Christmas cards which she offered for sale. Later she began to paint on boards, cookie-sheets, even the iron stove and walls. Eventually she painted the door of their tiny house with bright flowers, and decorated the windows and blinds as well. Her house was alive with her gaily painted birds, flowers and butterflies. Her oil paintings are generally small and bright, with paints applied directly from the tube rather than mixing of colours. In her later years visitors began to buy her paintings and even place orders for work.

Ref: Folk Art of Nova Scotia; Julie Watson, 'Primitive Painter'
Coll: Art Gallery of Nova Scotia; National Museum of Man (CCFCS)

LINDNER, MORITZ (1816-1898)
Toymaker   Berlin (Kitchener), Ontario
An immigrant from Germany, he opened a shop in Berlin, advertising toys, Christmas ornaments and Santa Claus figures which he made on the premises. His rocking-horses and children's sleighs are distinguished by bright dappled paint-decoration and stencilling.

Ref: Alfred Schenk, unpublished thesis
Coll: Doon Pioneer Village; Joseph Schneider Haus

LITZGUS, HAZEL (active 1970s and after)
Painter   Lloydminster, Alberta
This self-taught artist painted watercolour pictures based upon memories of her youth on the prairie farm near Lloydminster. She is particularly known for a watercolour depiction of herself, as a child, strolling down the road in the company of her mother, all set against a background of fields, forest and a road disappearing over the hills into a distant horizon.

Ref: Harper, *People's Art* (catalogue)

LOCHBAUM, JOSEPH (active 1830s, 1840s)
Fraktur artist   Markham area, Ontario
Known also as the 'Cumberland Valley Artist' or 'Nine Hearts Artist', this practitioner was active in both Pennsylvania and Ontario. He produced numerous hand-drawn birth-and-baptismal certificates in the Cumberland Valley area, before travelling north to York County, Upper Canada. He may have been a schoolteacher in the Markham area, where he inscribed records

Logan, Clarence (active 1960s and after). *Happy Birthday* U.S.A..
Painted wood: 1976.

for Mennonite settlers during the 1820s and 1830s. The design of his
certificates is unique, with text lettered within an arrangement of nine
hearts. His name is known from two signed examples, one in Pennsylvania,
the other in Ontario. Lochbaum's stay in Canada may have been brief, since
there exists no later information as to his whereabouts. At least two other
Markham-area artists copied or modified his style in fraktur certificates
drawn in the 1840s and 1850s.

Inf: Pastor Frederick S. Weiser
Ref: Bird, *Ontario Fraktur*; Bird and Kobayashi, A *Splendid Harvest*
Coll: Markham District Historical Museum

LODOEN, JEANETTE (active mid-20th century)
   Painter   Saskatoon, Saskatchewan
An amateur artist, she was born at Blaine Lake, northwest of Saskatoon. She
studied at the University of Saskatchewan, taking night classes, and is basi-
cally self-taught, painting landscapes and anecdotal subjects.

Ref: Saskatchewan Arts Board
Coll: Saskatchewan Arts Board

LOGAN, CLARENCE (active 1960s and after)
    Woodcarver   Havelock, Ontario
He carved humorous, often satirical figures, many of politicians. One of his
best-known works is a marionette of Jean Chretien, when he was Minister
of Finance, holding a box of Band-aids with which he undertook his patch-
work mending of the Canadian economy. He made wooden signs for a living, but indicated that his real avocation was that of carving caricatures of
public figures. A colourful 'Happy Birthday U.S.A.' motto made in 1976 for
the American Bicentennial is typical of plaques which he carved on
special occasions.

Ref: National Museum of Man Archives (CCFCS)

LOHNES, ALBERT (1895-1977)
    Knitter   West Berlin, Queens County, Nova Scotia
He spent most of his life on fishing vessels off the coast of Nova Scotia and
Massachusetts, where he nearly lost a hand due to infection. Around age 30
he devised an ingenious solution to the problem of a captain who com-
plained that he kept sliding around in his chair – Albert knitted a covering
for the seat. Around 1969 or 1970 he returned to this idea once again, but
now as an artistic pastime, having been recently forced into retirement due
to knee trouble encountered while sailing off Gloucester, Massachusetts. In
his late years he made decorative knitted covers for some 15 to 20 chairs,
many with pictorial designs and geometric elements, before having to give
up the hobby as a result of ill health.

Ref: Folk Art of Nova Scotia; From the Heart
Coll: Art Gallery of Nova Scotia; National Museum of Man (CCFCS)

LONEY, WILLIAM G. (1878-1956)
    Woodcarver   South Bay, Prince Edward County, Ontario
A blacksmith and general handyman, he engaged himself in a wide variety
of carving and constructing of objects, including birdhouses, weathervanes,
dioramas, tableaux of birds in marshland settings or various animal groupings. He also did oil paintings of both domestic and exotic subjects. Among
his finest carvings are acrobats on horseback and various circus performers.

Lohnes, Albert (1895-1977). Crocheted chair. Jute / wool and wood: 1965-75.
Coll: National Museum of Man (CCFCS).

Ref: From the Heart; Fleming, 'William G. Loney'; Harper, *People's Art* (catalogue)
Coll: National Museum of Man (CCFCS)

LORRAINE, PAUL (active 1930s and 1940s)
Decoy carver   Verdun, Québec
Among the second generation of Verdun carvers, Paul Lorraine made many
ducks of simple construction, design and painted decoration. His decoys are
frequently signed, and have been found throughout wide regions of
southwestern Québec.

Ref: Kangas and Kangas, *Decoys: A North American Survey*

LOUISON, MAURICE (1945-   )
Painter   Broadview, Saskatchewan
A capable painter, his sole instruction occurred while a student at Balfour
Collegiate. He lives on a Reserve near Broadview and has done paintings of
local countryside and familiar landmarks in the Broadview vicinity.

Ref: Saskatchewan Arts Board
Coll: Saskatchewan Arts Board

LUNNEAU, CLAUDE PIERRE (active 1960s and after)
Woodcarver   Toronto, Ontario
From his years of experience working as a crate-builder for museums and art
galleries, he had occasion to observe artifacts from the world over. Eventually he began to carve and construct works, sometimes basing these upon
mythological or popular themes. An example of his approach is his work
entitled 'Venus', inspired by a poem which contains a reference to a lady on
a mountain who needs a fine young man. Lunneau has interpreted the line
by placing a lady on the heights of a cage in which two wrestlers struggle to
win her affection.

Ref: From the Heart
Coll: National Museum of Man (CCFCS)

MACDONALD, CHARLES (active late 19th & early 20th centuries)
Cement sculptor, painter   Centreville, Nova Scotia
A craftsman working in a wide diversity of media, he did painting, wood-
carving, sculpting in cement, construction and assemblage. Among themes

Loney, William G. (1878-1956). Circus Acrobat on Horse. Painted wood:
early 20th century.

which he treated in sculpture form are Indians and scenes of Indian life, while paintings tend to be of familiar Nova Scotia views, landscapes and seascapes. Others include portraits and imitations of the work of Cornelius Krieghoff.

Ref: National Museum of Man Archives (Thomas Lackey file) (CCFCS)

MACDONALD, THOMAS (active 1820s and 1830s)

Painter   Hampstead, New Brunswick

An itinerant portrait artist, he travelled through the Gagetown and Fredericton areas of south central New Brunswick, doing watercolour paintings of prominent individuals and their families. In most cases, he places sitters against neoclassical backdrops, most likely in imitation of the conventions of formal portrait painters of the late 18th and early 19th centuries. He may have been inspired by the miniatures of J.H. Gillespie or other English artists who made periodic visits to Nova Scotia and New Brunswick to set up studio and do commissioned or advertised work. Macdonald was also an expert calligrapher and produced several illuminated genealogies for leading families of New Brunswick.

Ref: Bird, *Canadian Folk Art*; Dobson and Dobson; A *Provincial Elegance*; Harper, *A People's Art*
Coll: Queen's County Museum, Gagetown, New Brunswick

MACKIE, DAVID D. (1924-   )

Model maker   Edwards, Ontario

Born near Blackburn in Carleton County, he moved in 1961 up to Edwards, working on a farm. He made a variety of miniature vehicles in his leisure time, particularly hay carts, potato diggers and other implements which were eventually replaced by modern farm machinery.

Ref: National Museum of Man Archives (CCFCS)

MACLELLAN, CAPTAIN 'PEARLY' (active early 20th century)

Woodcarver   Port Grenville, Nova Scotia

Like many sea captains, 'Pearly' MacLellan found an artistic outlet during his leisure time, in which he carved or constructed numerous small furnishings and whimsies for friends and for his own family. He is especially known for a highly unusual desk featuring a carved masculine head,

MISS FRANCES PETERS ✳ MERRITT.

Macdonald, Thomas (active 1820s and 1830s). *Miss Frances Peters Merritt.*
Watercolour on paper: June 3, 1830.

reminiscent of a ship's figurehead, inscribed 'from father to Anna Bell'.

Ref: Decorated Nova Scotia Furnishings; From the Heart
Coll: National Museum of Man (CCFCS)

MACLELLAND, WILLIAM (active mid-20th century)
　　Woodcarver　　　　　　　　　　　　Ward's Brook, Nova Scotia
He carved highly varied figures, among them several amorous couples as well
as standing and kneeling human figures, boat models and carved figures. For
many years he worked as a ship's wright and rigger at the boat yards around
Port Graville, Nova Scotia. His later works were notably inspired by magazines and pin-up pictures.

Ref: National Museum of Man Archives (Thomas Lackey file) (CCFCS)

MACNEILL, ARTHUR (1926-　　)
　　Woodcarver　　　　　　　　　　　　St. Peter's, Prince Edward Island
A barber's son who did leather working, Arthur MacNeill took up carving
early in life, using shoe ink for colouration and drawing. One of his first
works was a bust of Abraham Lincoln which he carved from wood with his
mother's butcher knife. He also executed many drawings – maps, sketches,
coloured pencil compositions. He carved and painted small human figures in
settings such as school classrooms or domestic contexts.

Ref: National Museum of Man Archives (CCFCS)

MACWHIRTER, GAVIN H. (1894-　　)
　　Woodcarver　　　　　　　　　　　　New Richmond, Québec
Macwhirter was active for many years as a farmer who worked land at the
north end of the Cascapedia River. Late in life he developed carving as a pastime, making birds, multiple whirligigs and other works for his own
enjoyment.

Ref: National Museum of Man Archives (CCFCS)

MAHONIN, JOHN (active c. 1910-1930s)
　　Tinsmith, metal worker　　　　　　　　Veregin, Saskatchewan
As the influx of Doukhbors from Russia led to the establishment of villages
in western Canada, there arose the need for community buildings and

Maka, Jahan (1900-   ). *The Provinces*. Oil on canvas: c. 1975. Coll: National Museum of Man (CCFCS).

prayer-houses. John Mahonin was called upon to create elaborate decorative tinwork arcades for gables and porches of several structures, the most remarkable example being the community home at Veregin. The tin arches around this building feature fine fretwork designs in the form of lilies and other floral motifs.

Ref: Bird, *Canadian Folk Art*; Tarasoff, A *Pictorial History of the Doukhobors*
Coll: Veregin Doukhobor Museum

MAKA, JAHAN (1900-   )
    Painter   Flin Flon, Manitoba
Perhaps few folk artists endured the hardships which beset this self-taught painter. Born in Lithuania, he experienced extraordinary difficulties at a young age. His father had died when Jahan was only 13, leaving him as head

of the household. At age 14 he was conscripted into a Lithuanian cavalry squadron serving the Czar before the Russian Revolution. At the age of 27 he left war-ravaged Lithuania, enticed by stories of untold wealth and opportunity in Canada, reported by zealous immigration agents. He reached Canada just before the onset of the Great Depression. For 13 years he worked variously as a farmhand in Drumheller, Alberta, cutting trees in British Columbia, labouring in Regina and Winnipeg. In 1940 he became a miner at Sheridan, Manitoba, but was injured and returned to Winnipeg to recuperate. He later became a driller and then a hardrock miner at Flin Flon, retiring in 1965. He began painting in the late 1960s, depicting scenes from Flin Flon, the north, other cities he had visited, memories of Lithuania, family scenes, his mother's burial, the farm and the war. Occasionally he treated contemporary political and news events, from Muhammad Ali to Watergate. His work suggests a child-like style, with disregard or unawareness of natural perspective and interrelationship of details. Many of his works appear to represent his imagined view of unfamiliar places (Africa) and events (the first settlement of Canada), as in his portrayal of Asians discovering Canada and arriving on the 'Bering Strait Railway'.

Ref: From the Heart; Winnipeg Free Press (June 6, 1978)
Coll: National Museum of Man (CCFCS)

MANDAGGIO, EDWARD

new Carver and Painter   Near Bridgewater, Nova Scotia
Born Manitoba, May 4, 1927, Edward Mandaggio worked in northern Manitoba and Ontario as a trapper and as a hunting and fishing guide. He came to Nova Scotia in 1951, where he worked for the railroad for eight years, and since has worked in the lumber woods. He began carving around 1974, and painting around 1976 in order to liven up his cabin. Oxen, horses, roosters and human heads are some of his subjects. His work is among the most primitive of Nova Scotia Folk Art.

Inf: Chris Huntington

MANZER, DONALD (1912-)

Woodcarver   Ashmore, Digby Co., Nova Scotia
Don began carving in 1975. His first pieces were small oxen and other animals. He quickly expanded the size of his work and started making life-size animals and people. His work includes kangaroos, jackalopes, cats, dogs,

skunks, chickens, turkeys, rabbits, bears, an organ grinder, golfer, Robin Hood, a baker, a Mountie, a mailman, a baseball player, musicians, and many other subjects. He is one of Nova Scotia's best-known and most successful folk artists. Earlier in life he worked for the Department of Highways and as a farmer. Recently, he has retired as a school bus driver.

Coll: Art Gallery of Nova Scotia; National Museum of Man (CCFCS); Nova
   Scotia Art Bank; Represented Houston North Gallery
Inf: Chris Huntington

'MARITIME FAMILY RECORD ARTIST' (active 1830s)
   Calligrapher   New Brunswick
Unknown by name, an active itinerant scrivener travelled widely throughout the Maritimes and inscribed genealogical charts for families in New Brunswick and, to a lesser extent, Nova Scotia. His family registers are recognizable by numerous common features of handwriting, crowns and other decorative motifs.

Ref: Field, *Maritime Memorials* (typescript)
Coll: National Museum of Man (CCFCS)

MARKLE, GEORGE (active 1970s and after)
   Woodcarver   Medicine Hat, Alberta
In his leisure time following retirement, George Markle devoted his energy to carving animals and whimseys of various kinds. While many of his works are simple exercises in whittling, some examples are carved in the round with considerable richness of detail.

Ref: *Playful Objects*

MARKS, ADANIGA 'NIGEL' (active in late nineteenth century)
   Decoy carver   Margate, Prince Edward Island
Many decoys from Prince Edward Island are associated with the large geese and brant which abound there. Both flat-bottomed floating decoys and ones mounted on supports ('stick-ups') for planting in the ground are known to have been made by Adaniga 'Nigel' Marks in the late 19th century. A wagon and sleigh-maker, he made large decoys featuring carved, crossed wing tips, and he carved birds in various positions – preening, sleeping, feeding or swimming.

Ref: Kangas and Kangas, *Decoys: A North American Survey*

MARLATT, JOHN MILLS (active 1859-1868)
    Potter   Paris, Ontario
After a brief period of making earthenware at a small pottery at the village
of Oakland from 1857-59, he undertook a more substantial enterprise at Paris.
Here he produced stoneware crocks and jugs, and for a short period made
containers with blue floral decoration.

Ref: Newlands, *Early Ontario Potters*

MARTIN, S.W. (active c. 1842)
    Painter   London, England
The Canadian significance of this English artist lies in the fact that he advertised his work in the 1840s in the newspapers of Charlottetown, Prince
Edward Island. His business advertising was not without results, in that he
did receive at least a small number of Canadian commissions, a known example being a painting entitled 'Home from the Wood'.

Ref: Harper, *People's Art* (catalogue)

MARTINEAU, LIEUTENANT (active 1876)
    Illustrator   Manitoba
Lieutenant Martineau was a member of the Manitoba Mounted Police and
proved himself a capable amateur illustrator. In the 1870s he published
sketches of Pelly, Northwest Territory, appearing in *Canadian Illustrated News*.

Ref: Harper, *Painters and Engravers*
Coll: Royal Ontario Museum (Sigmund Samuel Canadiana Collection)

MAXCY, L. (active late 18th century)
    Gravestone carver   Salem, Massachusetts
Maxcy was a New England stonecutter whose work is known in Canada by
several examples of his workmanship in Nova Scotia cemeteries.

Ref: Trask, *Life How Short*

McCargar, W.C. (1906-   ). *Winter Sentinel*. Oil, crayon on panel: c. 1960.

McCAIRNS, ROBERT (active 1970s and after)
    Woodcarver   Turkey Point, Ontario
His carvings are highly diverse in subject and detail. A carver of numerous
species of birds, he has made many which are mounted on bases. Among his
many varieties are carved and painted ducks, woodpeckers, owls and shorebirds. He did many decoy and other bird carvings. The birds are for the most
part free interpretations and do not possess the literalness of the decoys.

Ref: National Museum of Man Archives (Thomas Lackey file) (CCFCS);
    Waddington's catalogue (October 6-7, 1981); Waddington's catalogue
    (June 15-17, 1980)

McCARGAR, W.C. (1906-   )
    Painter   Regina, Saskatchewan
Like several of his fellow naive painters, McCargar was born in Ontario (at
Newcastle, east of Toronto), and moved west at a young age. He was a self-
taught artist, and began to paint actively in 1958, beginning as a hobby for
self-amusement. His neighbour, Ken Lochhead, suggested that he throw his

paint-by-number kit out the window and do his own as something that would 'be more fun'. The artist Lochhead advised McCargar not to take painting lessons, and to develop his own style. In his own description, McCargar indicates that his artistic interest lay in recording his life's work, including his jobs on the railroad and on the farm. Many of his pictures are anecdotal, while a tone of nostalgia permeates most. Some works are simple observations of the immediate world of implements, stores and grain elevators, frequently shown in the background, toward which the eye follows strongly converging fences, railroad tracks or roads. Typical subjects are suggested by the titles 'The Old Steamer' and 'Winter Sentinel', depicting a towering grain elevator against the white snowbound prairie landscape.

Ref: Grassroots Saskatchewan catalogue; Prairie Folk Art
Coll: Saskatchewan Arts Board; National Museum of Man (CCFCS)

McKENDRY, PAT (c. 1915-   )
   Woodcarver   Orillia and Muskoka area, Ontario
Born near Orillia in Simcoe County, he was a loner who led a rustic existence. He lived in a barn for much of his life. Around 1960 he moved to the Muskoka wilderness and built himself a shack in the bush. Here he used his idle time to carve large birds and animals. Among these are depictions of events or activities involving animals, including a grizzly bear with a fish, a black bear, ground hog, fish, roosters, hawks, vultures and other creatures.

Ref: National Museum of Man Archives (CCFCS)

McLAUGHLIN, AGNES (c. 1920-   )
   Painter   Saint John, New Brunswick
When she took up painting as a hobby late in life, Agnes McLaughlin was returning to an interest which she had developed as a child. She had made numerous watercolour pictures which delighted her mother to the extent that they were put on display all over the house. This early talent was set aside upon the death of her mother and the necessity of having to care for her father and other family members. She worked for most of her life, then began to paint once again upon retirement and a move to New Brunswick from her Ontario home. Despite some art lessons, she is essentially a self-taught painter. Her later works are done in oil on canvas. Among subjects treated are landscapes, still-life pictures, scenes from farm life, fishing and activities in Saint John. She has also depicted a significant number of religious

McNeilledge, Alexander (1791-1874). *Confederation Box*. Painted wood: 1867.

subjects, frequently mingling a biblical story with a contemporary situation. Other paintings are nostalgic recollections of her personal upbringing, or of work, play and market scenes in Saint John.

Ref: Percival, 'The Folk Paintings of Agnes McLaughlin'

McNEILLEDGE, CAPTAIN ALEXANDER (1791-1874)
   Painter   Port Dover, Ontario

Born at Greenock, on the River Clyde, Scotland, the young Alex was introduced at an early age to life on the high sea. When only eight years old he accompanied his father, a sea captain, on an ocean voyage to Newfoundland. In subsequent years he was to work his way up from cabin helper to logkeeper and eventually captain. In his log he recorded weather conditions, celestial phenomena and dramatic events from shipwreck to piracy on journeys to China, Africa and the West Indies. By 1818 he was established in Philadelphia, marrying MaryAnn Thum in the next year. At the prodding of his brother Collin, he settled at Port Dover (then Dover Mills) on the Lake Erie shoreline in Upper Canada. Never successful at the clerking or farming which he attempted for several years, he wrote repeatedly and nostalgically of his sea-faring days long since left behind. In the 1840s he drew up a navigation chart based upon his travels with other captains around Lake Erie, a document used widely until the early 20th century. In his later years he began to make drawings of ships which he presented as tokens of friendship to captains of visiting vessels, as well as to relatives and neighbours. These drawings were personalized by naming the ship after the wife, the master after the husband, and smaller vessels after children. Most were accompanied by captions depicting fanciful and fictitious voyages, and many were inscribed with humourous autobiographical comments, a typical description being, 'Done in his 74th year / Wear no specks / Use no tobacco / Take only a wee drop as required / Not bad for an old Scotchie'. In a many-volumed diary which he maintained over the last 37 years of his life, he records not only routine daily events but also many personal feelings of frustration, loneliness and nonacceptance. The captain was found by his wife on August 21, 1874, having taken his life in the ravine behind the house the previous day.

Ref: Barrett, *Legend and Lore of Long Point*; Bird, *Canadian Folk Art*; Harper, *A People's Art*; Kobayashi et al, *Folk Treasures of Historic Ontario*
Coll: Eva Brook Donly Museum; National Gallery of Canada

McTAVISH, ROBERT (1888-1966)
　Woodcarver　　　　　　　　　　　　　　　　West Luther, Ontario
An older retired farmer in Wellington County, this amateur craftsman of Scottish extraction was from his youth familiar with the sight of horse-drawn buggies carrying Mennonites to and from home. From the 1950s on there began to develop a secondary settlement of Old Order Mennonites near the home of Robert McTavish, particularly as more and more Mennonite farmers began to purchase lands in Wellington County as Waterloo Conty farmland became less available. Observing his neighbours, Robert McTavish began to carve and construct horse-drawn buggies with Older Mennonite and Amish figures riding inside.

Ref: *Folk Art in Canada* (catalogue)
Coll: National Museum of Man (CCFCS)

MELANÇON (active 1840s)
    Painter   Québec
Little is known of the identity of this amateur artist, whose name is written
on the back of an oil portrait, dated 1846. This wonderfully naive painting
depicts the little girl Hermelène Laflamme, who later married into the
renowned Cartier family in Québec.

Ref: Harper, A *People's Art*

MELANSON, LAWRENCE (1916-   )
    Woodcarver   Mill Village, Nova Scotia
A carpenter by trade, he spent his entire life in Mill Village, carving in his
leisure time. Much of his work was inspired by popular images from the
media, calendars and popular art. A 'Dart Girl' which he made while working in a lumber camp in the 1950s was copied from a calendar pin-up. The
fact that it originally sat on a stand with an 8-day clock from an old Cadillac
indicates the degree to which Lawrence Melanson integrated hand-crafted
objects with mass-produced articles of the day.

Ref: From the Heart
Coll: National Museum of Man (CCFCS)

MELVIN, PHILIP (1938-   )
    Woodcarver   Ontario
Philip Melvin has led very much a 'down-and-out' existence throughout
much of his life. He was born at Lamanche, Newfoundland, and after arriving at Toronto described himself as 'the biggest fool that ever hit Toronto'
and as 'the man from Lamanche'. Finding himself in continual trouble with
the law and at the periphery of society, he spent a good deal of time in
correctional facilities or rehabilitation centres. At certain times he would
turn to carving and poetry, perhaps as a form of consolatory expression. In
1980 he began carving religious plaques and subjects, as well as painting
Toronto landmarks and familiar sights. For a time he was taken in at the
retreat house at Combermere, where the nuns looked after him. Some of
his religious carving is undoubtedly a thankful response to the kindness of
these and other church people. He carved a dark-skinned nun, probably an
image of Mother Theresa, an Indian Princess looking upon the Miracle of
the Cross and other religious works, some accompanied by poetry. He also
carved an elaborate diorama depicting an incident involving a wrecked ship,

for which he provided a lengthy accompanying story in handwritten form.
Spending time at the Lakehead, or in Toronto, often at St. Michael's
Cathedral, Philip Melvin would sometimes turn to carving in hope of selling
a few pieces as a means of minimal survival.

Inf: Ralph and Patricia Price
Ref: From the Heart
Coll: National Museum of Man (CCFCS)

MIGNAULT, ABBÉ JOSEPH (active c. 1936)
   Sculptor   Québec
Reputedly a teacher of natural history, this artist is known by a diorama
featuring an owl and background assembled from plants and feathers,
believed to have been used for school demonstration purposes. Its composition suggests a degree of familiarity with problems of perspective and proportion, indicating the possibility that the artist may have been
a painter as well.

Ref: Harper, People's Art (catalogue)

MILBURN (active c. 1860)
   Painter   Western Ontario
This rather accomplished amateur painter is known principally on the basis
of an oil painting, showing the railway locomotive The Saxon, which ran
between Hamilton aand London, Ontario.

Ref: Harper, A People's Art
Coll: McIntosh Art Gallery, University of Western Ontario, London, Ontario

MILL, WILLIAM ROY (1901-   )
   Decoy carver   Mill Point and Kensington, Prince Edward Island
One of the most prolific of Maritime carvers, William Roy Mill was born on
Mill Point and later lived at Kensington. His carving career began in 1934
when he made several geese decoys of considerable artistic merit. Although
he was to carve numerous species, his favourite subject was the goose. With
increasing market demand for his work, he began to simplify his later goose
models. He is considered to have pioneered the practise of using three metal
spikes as legs to support goose decoys. Most are field geese, rather than
floaters, typically in an upright or feeding position,

with skillful feather-painted decoration.

Ref: Guyette and Guyette, *Decoys of Maritime Canada*

150   MITCHELL, JANET (1915-   )
      Painter   Calgary, Alberta
An amateur painter, she was born at Medicine Hat, and began drawing in
her youth. She had a few lessons at the Banff Summer School of Art in 1942,
but remains essentially self-taught. Her work is characterized by a somewhat
naive style, as evident in her oil-on-board or oil-on-canvas paintings of
landscapes, skies and scenes based on Alberta geography or her imagination.
Her large pictures are described by titles such as 'Moon over Mountain Village' or 'Celestial Night'.

Ref: National Gallery of Canada Archives
Coll: National Gallery of Canada

MONGRAIN, YVETTE (1929-   )
      Yard artist   St-Stanislas, Champlain County, Québec
Typical of many yard artists, her work is interesting not only in its individual
pieces but as an environmental composition. Her groupings suggest humour,
whimsy, imagination, fantasy and other moods. Using found materials,
including bottles, lanterns, wheels, cutlery, plastic flowers and other discarded items, she has created individual sculptural forms and tableaux,
embellishing the walls of her house and front yard.

Ref: les patenteux du Québec

MONKS, KENNETH (1879-   )
      Furniture maker, carpenter King's Cove, Bonavista Bay, Newfoundland
Kenneth Monks was a sufficiently capable woodcarver and builder that he
was hired to work on the interior of St. James Anglican Church at King's
Cove in 1896. His skillful fretwork carving appears in both architecture and
furniture, notably a uniquely styled bed with Gothic arch and tracery. He
was equally competent in the art of lettering, as evident in signs which he
painted, and in the motto which he created over the chancel of St. James.

Ref: Peddle, *The Traditional Furniture of Outport Newfoundland*
Coll: Newfoundland Museum

MOORES, ANDREW JACKSON (1900-1976)
    Woodcarver   Mitton, Nova Scotia
A retired fisherman and worker at various odd jobs, he had always enjoyed
whittling as a pastime. In later life he expended greater energy and time in
this pursuit, carving crooked knives and walking sticks, some with ornate   151
handles worked in the shapes of rooster heads and various animals.

Ref: Peter Barss, *Older Ways: Nova Scotia Traditional Craftsmen*

MOORES, CLARENCE (1925-   )
    Woodcarver   Milton, Nova Scotia
Son of Andrew Jackson Moores, he is known variously as Clarence, or
'Bubby' Moores. He took up woodcarving late in life, during times of
reduced work at the paper mill in Brooklyn, Nova Scotia. His initial efforts
were of modest proportion, mostly in the form of small whittled crooked
knives. Clarence began to carve a man, and wound up completing it as a
woman, naming the piece 'Penelope'. Because of the large size of most of his
sculptures, he was forced to use several planks laminated together to give
sufficient thickness. Typically he would start by cutting out a rough outline
with a chain saw, then work down to a hammer and chisel, finishing with a
belt sander. His carvings are very much a prduct of the powertool age. He
followed the carving of Penelope by creating a boxer, and which Clarence
named Ulysses. He carved numerous individual pieces and also pairs or
groups of embracing and dancing figures, many of which he placed in his yard.

Ref: Folk Art of Nova Scotia; Waddington's catalogue (June 15-17, 1980)

MOREL, OCTAVE (active late 19th century)
    Woodcarver   Québec City, Québec
This carver received many commissions for church figures and relief-carving
of tabernacle doors and altar fronts. He also undertook a wide variety of
ornamental carving for himself and those in the community wishing to place
orders with him. His work is represented in the elaborate carving of boxes
and furniture, as well as numerous smaller works which stand somewhat
apart from the formality of his religious carving.

Ref: Lessard and Marquis, *French-Canadian Antiques*; National Museum of Man
    Archives (CCFCS)
Coll: National Museum of Man (CCFCS); Québec Museum

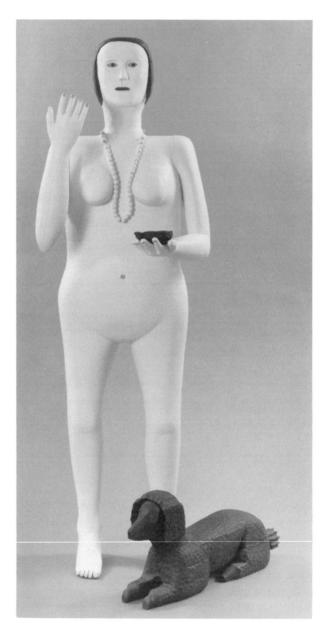

Moores, Clarence (1925-   ). *'Penelope' and Poodle*. Painted wood: 1976. Coll:
National Museum of Man (CCFCS).

MORIN, JOSEPH (active early 20th century)
    Woodcarver   Québec
Little is known of the personal life of this carver, apart from an elaborately
embellished folk art 'Love Box' carved and decorated by him. The fairly skillful quality of the piece suggests that he may have done considerable carving.   153

Ref: Canadian Antiques and Art Review (December / January 1980 / 81)

MORRISSEY, MICHAEL (active early 20th century)
    Furniture maker   Riverhead, Harbour Grace, Newfoundland
While recuperating at a tubercular sanatorium near St. John's c. 1915,
Michael Morrissey took up whittling and the making of simple furniture as a
pastime. Several chairs reveal his considerable ingenuity in carved rungs, spin-
dles and posts, sometimes done in imitation of sophisticated rope-carving.
Other chairs, especially rockers, feature rustic decoration in the form of simple shaping, scrollwork and chip-carving.

Ref: Peddle, *The Traditional Furniture of Outport Newfoundland*

MORRISON, A.L. (1909-   )
    Painter   Pleasant Grove, Prince Edward Island
Alfred L. Morrison was of the sixth generation of Morrisons on Prince
Edward Island. His love of history was engendered by early encounters with
Father MacMillan's *History of the Catholic Church in Prince Edward Island* and
Campbell's *History of the Island*. Personal dissatisfaction with technological
change and the consequent loss of appreciation of old ways led him to the
conviction that he should write a personal history of Island life, and a deci-
sion to write an elementary school textbook, starting with a history of
Grand Tracadie. The sudden appearance in 1963 of a government-sponsored
publication by two Halifax writers put an end to Alfred's project. Rather
than dropping the idea altogether, however, he began to consider painting
as an alternative means by which to tell the story of Prince Edward Island.
Apart from drafting instruction in high school and a non-credit visit to an art
course taught by a personal friend, he had no formal artistic training.
Morrison's paintings are oil-on-canvas depictions of historical events, from
the 'birth of the island' (shown as a direct act of God!) to early discoveries,
battles, shipwrecks, pioneer settlements, the proclamation of

Morrison, Alfred L. (1909-   ). *Birth of the Island*. Oil on hardboard: 1967.

Confederation and farm scenes prior to changes brought by mechanization.

Ref: A.L. Morrison, *My Island Pictures*

MORTON, JUSTUS
   Potter   Brantford, Ontario
He is known to be the founder of the pottery at Brantford in 1849, making
him possibly the earliest stoneware potter in Ontario. Emigrating from
Lyons, New York, where he had probably earlier practised his trade, Morton
produced blue-decorated stoneware, as well as numerous decorative pieces
featuring applied flowers, birds and classical motifs.

Ref: Newlands, *Early Ontario Potters*; Webster, *Early Canadian Pottery*
Coll: Royal Ontario Museum (Sigmund Samuel Canadiana Collection)

MORTON, LEO (-1979)
   Woodcarver   Barss Corner, Lunenburg Co., Nova Scotia
Leo worked as a woodsman and for some years operated a tug pulling the

log booms for the Mersey Mill in Liverpool. He was a prolific and imaginative woodcarver, making elaborate whirligigs, birds, dancing men, and other figures. The tugboat was covered with his work, which he left behind when he retired.

Inf: Chris Huntington
Coll: Art Gallery of Nova Scotia

MOUGEOT-RABY MARGUERITE (c. 1930-   )

Painter   Thurso, Papineau County, Québec

Wife of a dairy farmer and the mother of four children, Marguerite Mougeot-Raby was nevertheless able to set aside time to devote energy to painting as a pastime. She did not confine her work to paper or canvas, however, and soon undertook the ambitious project of painting large plywood panels as decorative scenes for the barns and other buildings of the farmstead. Her large works, painted with outdoor house paints, feature rural scenes and portraits of domestic animals. In 1980 her painting of a sheep was exhibited at the Papineauville Fair to publicize sheep-raising in the county.

Ref: From the Heart
Coll: National Museum of Man (CCFCS)

MOULDING, FRED (1894-   )

Woodcarver   Regina, Saskatchewan

A hard-working farmer who endured the hardships of the Depression and continual difficulties besetting the profession, he did not take up woodcarving until in his mid-60s, beginning to carve in earnest around 1960. His various carved and constructed scenes are not so much nostalgic as documentary, reflecting his statement that he thought younger people would not know much about the implements and techniques of farming from earlier days unless shown examples of some kind. His carved wagons, sleighs, plows and other articles are such examples. He used his artistic means to create scenes of daily life on the farm, including depictions of plowing, butchering, women's work and other aspects of early rural life. Although he carved many individual figures of deer, pheasants, badgers, buffalo, muskrats, grain wagons, roadbuilding equipment, buggies and stagecoaches, it is his groupings of figures and implements that reveal his interest in presenting visual history.

Ref: From the Heart; Grassroots Saskatchewan (catalogue); Prairie Folk Art
Coll: National Museum of Man (CCFCS); Saskatchewan Arts Board

MOYER, SAMUEL (1767-1844)
Fraktur artist   Lincoln County, Ontario

When thirty-three families left Bucks County, Pennsylvania, to meet the challenge of new opportunity in Upper Canada, the school teacher Samuel Moyer was among them, arriving at a spot near present-day Vineland in 1786. He is known to have been an expert calligrapher (a requirement of the Pennsylvania German school master) and fraktur artist. As the first teacher in the Mennonite school in Lincoln County, he is believed to be the artist who produced many of the beautifully-illuminated songbooks made and given to pupils there during the first decades of the 19th century. Many stylized drawings of similar workmanship, with tulips and birds, were probably made by Moyer as awards to students at the end of the school term each year in March or April. He is probably the earliest Ontario fraktur artist, and appears to have practised the artform at an earlier date while still in eastern Pennsylvania.

Ref: Bird, Ontario Fraktur; Bird and Kobayashi, A Splendid Harvest
Coll: Jordan Museum of The Twenty

MUNROE, GEORGE (1907-   )
Wood carver   Glace Bay, Cape Breton Co., Nova Scotia

George Munroe emigrated from England with his family at the age of seven. His first occupation was as ordinary seaman and later as a merchant marine. He is a veteran as an iron rigger of military ships during the second war. In late years he made a number of small painted figures of single or double men and women standing at lecturns, seated in rockers or in pairs on book-ends. He often applied purchased dogs from tea boxes to the bases of his work. All of his pieces have a delicate humour which is augmented by the fact that the hands of his figures are always jointed at the wrist.

Inf: Chris Huntington

MUYSSON, HERTHA (1898-1984)
Painter   Guelph, Ontario

The family background of Hertha Muysson was artistically very rich. Her father, Bertold Kirchner, had been an accomplished woodcarver in Berlin,

Muysson, Hertha (1898-1984). *Listening to the News*. Oil on canvas: c. 1970.

Germany. Hertha was herself highly skilled as a dressmaker. She did not take up painting until she was already 70 years of age, at which time she began to do oil portraits and other scenes on canvas. She painted frequently from direct observation or remembered impressions of neighbours, friends and family members. At other times she worked from other paintings, as in a picture of a small girl entitled 'Imaginary Portrait After Renoir'. Her background in the art of dressmaking was undoubtedly influential in her studied attention to details of clothing and the license she would sometimes take in selecting the 'best' coat or scarf for each sitter depicted. A distinctive feature in her portraiture is the use of strong colour-field backgrounds to accentuate faces. She also painted several self-portraits, one of which is a highly arresting picture of the artist 'listening to the news', hearing of a disastrous tidal wave which shattered dikes and inundated her beloved Dutch homeland.

Ref: The Imaginary Portrait; Kobayashi et al, Folk Treasures of Historic Ontario

MYATT, WALTER (1900-   )
    Carver   Chezzetcook, Halifax Co., Nova Scotia
Walter lives with his wife in an early little house in an Acadian village just east of Halifax. He began making life-size carvings of birds about 1974. Walter found that the sales of these picked up after being discovered by a TV crew canvassing the community to see what people were doing. He is fairly prolific and has recently made several life-sized chickens.

Inf: Chris Huntington

NADEAU, ALBERT (1919-   )
    Woodcarver   St. Francois, Madawaska County, New Brunswick
This self-taught artist began by carving as a form of self-amusement and eventually found himself carving consciously for the larger public. His first involvement took the form of whittling and carving during his teens as a farm boy, largely for his own enjoyment and somewhat later, at the request of friends. At the remarkably young age of 18 a number of his carved 'Studies from Life' were displayed at the Legislative Library at the Parliament Buildings in Fredericton. Among an enormous range of subjects which he treated were various animals, hunting scenes, plowing, sowing, water-carrying, blacksmithing and other forms of human labour. He carved many free-standing human figures, but is best known for his relief-carvings, many depicting familiar scenes or anecdotes, and an elaborate memorial to soldiers who had given their lives on the battlegrounds of World War One.

Ref: Daily Mail (Fredericton): April 15, 1937

'NEMO' (see DARLING, JAMES)

NICHOL, D.W. (1890-1977)
    Decoy carver   Smith's Falls, Ontario
Inspired by the work of two uncles who had carved decoys at an earlier date (A.D. Nichol and D.K. Nichol), Davy, or D.W. Nichol began carving at

an extremely early age. He is reported to have made decoys by age fifteen, and carved birds virtually until the time of his death in 1977. In his earlier years he produced many hunting decoys, while in later life he confined himself to showbirds made upon request. His decoys are distinguished by exceptionally fine painting, carving and a coggled detail on the head. The high artistic quality of his work influenced other decoy carvers in eastern Ontario.

Ref: Gates, *Ontario Decoys*

NICKERSON, FRED (1902-1980)
    Decoy carver   Reynoldscroft, Nova Scotia
Fred Nickerson is known in both Nova Scotia and Massachusetts, his decoys having been found in both regions. A boatbuilder at Villagedale, Nova Scotia, he reportedly carved the majority of his decoys there, and probably took some of these carvings with him to Massachusetts during a period of domicile at Cape Cod. Like other Nova Scotia carvers, he made decoys with long, low body profiles and relief-carved wings. He carved bluebills, whistlers, scoders and eiders, with his finest work being revealed in his merganser decoys.

Ref: Kangas and Kangas, *Decoys: A North American Survey*

NICKERSON, J.M. (active early 20th century)
    Painter   Vancouver, British Columbia
This amateur artist, about whom little is known, painted a large picture entitled *Princess May on Sentinel Island, Alaska, Aug. 5, 1912*. This oil on canvas work depicts a shipwreck on rocks off the Pacific coast, with its crew virtually suspended in the air looking down upon the rocks which have lifted the large vessel almost entirely out of the sea. Its naive sense of perspective and scale make it an exceptional example of primitive painting.

Ref: Harper, *A People's Art*
Coll: Vancouver City Archives

'NINE HEARTS ARTIST' (see LOCHBAUM, JOSEPH)

NORRIS, JOSEPH (1924-   )
    Painter   Lower Prospect, Nova Scotia
In his younger years he had worked as a fisherman and at construction work

Norris, Joe (1924-   ). Decorated chest. Painted wood: 1975. Coll: Art
Gallery of Nova Scotia.

at various places along the South Shore of Nova Scotia. Born at Halifax, much
of his early life had been characterized by illness, especially pleurisy. As a
consequence of his illness, he was confined, and did some painting to keep
himself occupied. A severe heart attack forced him into early retirement
from fishing. During his convalescence, at age 49, he was given artistic
encouragement from a visiting nurse who provided him with materials and
prodded him to do a little painting each day. Eventually he found that there
was enough interest developing in his work to support himself, a practice
which became still more frequent after he moved into a little yellow house
in Lower Prospect where he continued to paint on a daily basis. He took his

painting seriously to the extent of working long, hard days, but always put aside his brushes by 10:00 to watch late-night television programmes. His painting of gulls, animals, ships and landscapes began in conventional form, done in oil on canvas or panel. A rather unusual change of approach occurred when he began painting these subjects on the sides of storage boxes, on tables, chairs, and even chests of drawers. A bachelor, Joe Norris would indicate from time to time that he had missed certain things in life, and claim that painting was his consolation.

Ref: Folk Art of Nova Scotia; From the Heart; Pearse, 'Joe Norris'
Coll: Art Gallery of Nova Scotia; Dalhouse University Art Gallery; Mira
   Godard Gallery (One-Man Show); Houston North Gallery

NOWLAN, EMERY (1887-1982)

Woodcarver   Black River, Nova Scotia

A carpenter and vegetable farmer in Kings County, he first took up carving and painting after his retirement in the 1960s. He carved principally birds, sometimes depicted singly, or in clusters on 'trees' made from branches. He carved also squirrels, bears, some human figures, but concentrated for the most part on bird carvings. Although he may initially have indulged in his hobby for self-entertainment, from virtually the outset he sold carvings to visitors at his home in Black River.

Inf: Chris Huntington
Ref: Folk Art of Nova Scotia; Waddington's catalogue (June 21-22, 1982)

OBED, JESSE CLAYTON (1878-1932)

Decoy carver   Blanche, Nova Scotia

Jesse Obed was, like many other decoy makers, an active fisherman. In addition he later became lighthouse keeper at the Half Moon Lighthouse offshore from the town of Blanche. Most of his carving was undertaken in spare hours when working at the lighthouse. Principal Obed decoys include whistlers and eiders. Many feature well-carved bills and unusually smooth finishes, and are fitted with glass eyes. His decoys are both graceful and realistic, and his style was copied by numerous other carvers.

Ref: Guyette and Guyette, Decoys of Maritime Canada

O'BRIEN, MARY MARGARET (1905-   )
    Rug maker   Cape Broyle, Newfoundland
Mary O'Brien first undertook the project of mat hooking in her early years
when her husband Jim was busy on snowy days cutting wood or setting

snares in the forest. After his retirement, he began to assist his wife, drawing
designs and cutting up rags for her. Her hooked rugs are based almost
exclusively upon geometric designs, notably block and diamond patterns.

Ref: Memorial University Art Gallery, *The Fabric of their Lives*

O'CONNOR, PATRICK (c. 1890-1960)
    Woodcarver   Bob's Lake, Ontario
For most of his life Patrick O'Connor struggled as a farmer in north Fron-
tenac County. By his 60s he had turned increasingly to hobbies, the most
notable of which was perhaps his woodcarving interest. Around the middle
of the century he undertook the carving of many animals and human
figures. At first he carved bird's heads and human figures, singly, and then as
groupings. He created an elaborate miniature scene of two wrestlers which
functioned as a whirligig, as well as a group of small figures, assorted animals,
reptiles, a wolf's head, deer's head, an Indian, axes, a sulky and other miniatures. One of his most remarkable projects was a grouping of human heads,
each with varying facial expression, carved around 1950.

Ref: '*Twas Ever Thus*
Coll: National Museum of Man (CCFCS)

OSMOND, HUBERT (active 1960s and after)
    Yard artist   Cape Ray, Southwest Coast, Newfoundland
In his spare moments he found occasion to decorate the front of his house
and lawn in this coastal village. Like many yard artists, he created many
works from found materials, but was also a capable woodcarver, as evident
in a caribou head which he made using real antlers inserted into a head
which he carved by hand.

Ref: Memorial University Art Gallery, *Flights of Fancy*

PAGE, J.R. (active 1860s)
    Painter   Ottawa area, Ontario
Little is known of the life of this artist, except for an oil painting of a

pedigree shorthorn, reputedly from the Ottawa district. He is known to have sketched livestock for reproduction in *Canada Farmer*. His work is generally in the naive style.

Ref: Harper, *Painters and Engravers*; Harper, *People's Art* (catalogue)
Coll: McCord Museum

PANKO, WILLIAM (1892-1948)

Painter   Drumheller, Alberta

The Panko family migrated from Austria to Canada in 1911. Holder of many odd jobs, William worked in the Drumheller coal mines in winter and visited farms in summer. Most of his watercolour paintings were executed in later life, while recovering in a sanatorium from tuberculosis. His pictures generally recall earlier, happy days, although others present images of contemporary life in Drumheller and in other geographical places familiar to the artist. A number of Panko's paintings were exhibited in Calgary in the 1940s, making him among the earliest naive painters to gain public attention in English Canada.

Inf: George Swinton
Ref: Harper, A *People's Art*

PAQUETTE, JOSEPH (active c. 1900-1925)

Decoy carver   Verdun, Québec

One of the 'Verdun school' of carvers, Joseph Paquette produced decoys during the first third of the century. He made many varieties of ducks and geese of both solid and hollow-body types.

Ref: Kangas and Kangas, *Decoys: A North American Survey*

PARENT, HARVEY (1913-   )

Yard artist   Grande-Anse, Laviolette County, Québec

For many years he worked variously for Québec Hydro and near Indian reserves where he encountered many of the images which are incorporated in his art. He began in later years to whittle and carve faces, masks and a large totem pole over twelve feet in height. He drew upon mythology and pictures in books, as well as upon Indian folklore and ceremonial ritual in creating the many figures and designs on his house and lawn.

Ref: les patenteux du Québec

Patterson, Dan (1886-1968). *Cathedral*. Condensed milk tins: 1960s. Coll: National Gallery of Canada.

PARENT, LAUDA (1892-1977)
    Woodcarver   Templeton, Québec
Lauda Parent had been disabled by a gas attack during the First World War,
leaving him incapable of future work. With time on his hands, he immersed
himself in various hobbies, the dominant one being carving and construction   165
of models of many kinds. Using wood and other materials he made miniature trains, dirigibles and various other objects.

Ref: Folk Art in Canada (catalogue)
Coll: National Museum of Man (CCFCS)

PATTERSON, DAN (1886-1968)
    Sculptor   St. Thomas, Ontario
Although in his spare time Dan Paterson had always involved himself in making yard ornaments and decorations of one kind or another, all of these projects paled in comparison with a single undertaking which dominated his life
for several years. Collecting Carnation Milk cans from neighbours, friends
and institutions in the St. Thomas area, he worked in stages, constructing a
'Cathedral' inside his house, filling virtually the entire space of his living
room from wall to wall and floor to ceiling. With more than 2600 of these
containers he made arches, windows, columns, gothic vaults and other
details. After countless visits by curious local sightseers, arrangements were
made for this 'tin environment' to be taken down and re-assembled for
exhibition at an international show of folk art in Czechoslovakia in 1969,
before it was given a permanent home at the National Gallery of Canada
in Ottawa.

Inf: Tony Urquhart
Ref: University of Waterloo, Primitives and Folk Art
Coll: National Gallery of Canada

PAULS, HENRY (1904-   )
    Painter   Blythewood, Ontario
Henry Pauls was born in the Mennonite community at Chortitza, in South
Russia. In 1916 his family, along with many others, were subjected to harsh
persecution by Bolsheviks in the region, precipitating a mass exodus to
Canada and the United States. Henry migrated to Saskatchewan in 1923, followed by Sara, his bride-to-be, in 1927. They lived for many years near the
village of Sonningdale, before eventually moving to southern Ontario. After

retirement from tomato and vegetable gardening in the 1970s, Henry began to turn attention to the recording of his life in words and pictures. His oil paintings depict scenes of daily life in Russia (*My First Lesson in Mennonite History, Peter Hildebrand Writing His Memories, A Sunday Afternoon, Mennonites Going to Church*) or record farms and familiar landmarks (*The Administration Building, The Large Oak*, etc.). He also painted several pictures of life in Saskatchewan and Ontario, and a smaller number of hand-lettered religious mottoes with accompanying pictures.

Ref: Pauls, *The Story of Our Life in Words and Pictures*
Coll: Conrad Grebel College; National Museum of Man (CCFCS)

PAWLYK, KOST (1905-   )
    Yard artist   Elk Point, Alberta
Like many yard artists, Kost Pawlyk carved weathervanes and whirligigs of various types for placement around the exterior of his home. He tended to paint his various wind toys and garden ornaments in extremely bright colours, and on at least one example, a duck whirligig, decorated the pro-pellers with strong geometric designs reminiscent of those on textiles which he would have known from his Ukrainian background.

Ref: From the Heart
Coll: National Museum of Man (CCFCS)

PAYZANT (active late 19th century)
    Painter   Nova Scotia
Virtually nothing is known of the life of this artist, who is reputedly the painter of an oil portrait of an aging ship owner, done in oil. The work is rather skillful but essentially naive in execution, depicting a bearded entrepreneur at the prime of his commercial success with a background in which we see a large sailing ship, presumably belonging to the sitter.

Ref: Harper, A *People's Art*
Coll: Nova Scotia Museum

PENNEY, ROOSEVELT
    Woodcarver   South Side, Shelburne Co., Nova Scotia
Roy Penney is a middle-aged man primarily known as a decoy maker. He grew up in this fishing community and followed the fishery. He has made

interesting carvings of peacocks and partridges in the folk art vein.

Inf: Chris Huntington

PEPPER, NORMAN (active 1970s and after)

Neu   Yard artist   Hensall, Ontario
Having worked at many odd jobs in this Huron County community, Norman Pepper in later years began the project of transforming his house, sheds and lawn into a fanciful environment using a combination of found materials and designs which he would cut out from plywood and paint. He made numerous birdhouses, and decorated not only buildings but even trees with carved birds and animals, as well as constructing windmills, gates, weathervanes and whirligigs.

Inf: Norman Pepper

PERRON, ANGÈLE (active 1880s)
    Coverlet maker   Les Éboulements-en-Haut, Québec
This craftswoman exemplifies at its best a tradition centred in Charlevoix County, notably that of boutonné decoration of coverlets made in the region. Many of these unusual coverlets are immediately recognizable due to distinctive rows of geometric patterns worked in knots of wool. Angèle Perron's coverlet features, additionally, the figural representations of a man and woman (possibly bride and groom), suggesting that this piece was made for the occasion of a wedding.

Ref: Burnham and Burnham, *Keep Me Warm One Night*
Coll: National Gallery of Canada

PERRON, MARTIAL (active 1970s)
    Sculptor   Saint-Marc-des-Carrières, Québec
A woodcarver by avocation, Martial Perron began in the 1970s to use chalk as a medium for the carving of birds and animals. His works are primitive in their execution, but often feature remarkable details of workmanship with carving and painting to give texture. His work was chosen for a travelling exhibit of Québec folk art in 1975.

Ref: art populaires du Québec (catalogue)
Coll: Musée du Québec

Perron, Angèle (active 1880s). Boutonné coverlet. Wool on cotton: c. 1885.
Coll: National Gallery of Canada.

PETITOT, EMILE (1838-1917)

Painter   Northwest Canada

Father Petitot was born at Grancey-le-Château in France, and was sent to
Canada as a missionary to the Indians of the Northwest. He painted ship-
scenes and views of pioneer settlements during his travels. He is particularly
known for his oil painting depicting Fort Edmonton, the Hudson's Bay Company Post, eventually razed to make way for the Alberta Legislative Buildings and the growing city of Edmonton. He was a capable painter and illustrator, and his visit as a missionary for the Oblate Order in 1861 or 1862 made

Pickett, Sarah T. (active 1840s). *The Steamship Sarah*. Watercolour on paper: 1848. Coll: New Brunswick Museum.

him one of the first missionaries to work north of the Artic Circle. He painted numerous landscapes in primitive style, as well as some religious works, and decorated some of his chapels along the Mackenzie River with religious murals. He did a number of pen and ink and pencil sketches for books which he published on geography, anthropology and linguistics.

Ref: Harper, *Painters and Engravers*; Harper, A *People's Art*; Public Archives of Canada
Coll: Alberta Legislative Library; Edmonton Art Gallery

PICKET, SARAH T. (active 1848)
    Painter   Kingston, New Brunswick
Sarah Picket is known on the basis of work done as a child, at which age she had already displayed considerable talent. Her school exercise book, dated 1848, features numerous charming drawings of ships and calligraphy exercises, as well as decorative embellishments throughout. A particularly bold work, entitled 'The Steamship Sarah', features competent pen outlining and vibrant watercolours.

Ref: Harper, A *People's Art*
Coll: New Brunswick Museum

Pringle, Mary Ann, and Wallace, Agnes Pringle (active 1840s). *Queen Victoria*.
Embroidery and oil on silk: 1840s. Coll: Royal Ontario Museum.

PIEROWAY, PERCY (1921-   )
    Painter   St. George's and Stephenville, Newfoundland
A business administrator and enthusiastic participant in community organiza-
tions, Percy Pieroway first took up painting in the early 1970s. His various
works, mostly done in oil on fibre board, feature views of the land and seas-
cape of the St. George's area. His paintings were included in exhibits of
Newfoundland folk art held in St. John's in 1976 and 1977.

Ref: Memorial University, *Folk Images '77*
Coll: National Museum of Man (CCFCS)

POULIN, ANTOINETTE (1898-   )
    Yard artist   St-Edouard, Lotbinière
There was perhaps never a time in her life when Antoinette Poulin did not
paint, carve or make something of artistic interest. The impetus to decorate
her yard appears to have come after an occasion when, finding a dead canary
alongside a road in Maine, she had it mounted and displayed. She then
began gradually to build up an environment of small houses, boats, windmills, lighthouses and bridges in her yard, which she populated with her
hand-made small human figures, and even an 'orchestra' of stuffed squirrels
playing musical instruments which she made from various materials.

Ref: les patenteux du Québec

PREVOST, E. NELPHAS (1904-   )
    Woodcarver   Fassett, Québec
Born in Saint-Andreé-Avellin between Ottawa and Montréal, he did some
forms of whittling and carving from his youth. He spent his childhood working on the family farm, and later years in lumber camps, before eventually
securing regular employment at a mill. In his earlier years he carved animals,
often in sympathy with the shape of roots, branches or driftwood which he
would pick up in his travels. Later in life he began to make violins, carving
them from solid or laminated sections of pine. The interest in violin-making
was stimulated by a request from a neighbour, and no doubt recalled childhood familiarity with the instrument as played by members of his own family. Many of his violins featured incised or painted stars and geometric
motifs, or even an elaborate lion's head carved in place of the scroll. He also
made highly decorative cases.

Ref: From the Heart
Coll: National Museum of Man (CCFCS)

PRINGLE, MARY ANN McLEAN (active 1841)

Painter   St. Thomas, Ontario

An amateur artist, she is known particularly on the basis of an unusual work, a painting of Queen Victoria, with embroidery done by her daughter, Agnes Pringle Wallace (see WALLACE, AGNES PRINGLE).

Ref: Harper, A People's Art
Coll: Royal Ontario Museum (Sigmund Samuel Canadiana Collection)

PRINGLE, PETER M. (1880s-1950s)

    Decoy carver   Dunnville, Ontario

The carved birds known to have been made by Pete Pringle reveal an unusual competence and sensitivity to fine detail, perhaps a consequence of the fact that he was as well or even better-known as a lithograph engraver at Dunnville. His various ducks and other birds, most as solid sculptures, are finely carved and painted, and are sometimes considered to have been an inspiration for the later work of carver Ken Anger.

Ref: Gates, Ontario Decoys

RAMSAY, JOHN (1858-1934)

    Decoy carver   Summerside, Prince Edward Island

Of all Prince Edward Island decoy makers, John Ramsay is generally acknowledged to be the master. Early in life he worked at Hall Manufacturers, a threshing mill firm located in Summerside. In his 40s, he began to carve in earnest, making many varieties of geese and ducks. He created various action stances in his carving of geese and brant decoys, preening, poised for attack and other positions. In all, he is believed to have carved more than a thousand brant and goose decoys, including both floating and stick-up types. Ramsay decoys tend to exhibit little or no carved detail, but frequently exhibit outstanding painted finishes.

Ref: Guyette and Guyette, Decoys of Maritime Canada; Kangas and Kangas,
    Decoys: A North American Survey

RANDALL, HARRY (active 1970s and after)
    Yard artist   Trinity East, Trinity Bay, Newfoundland
Harry Randall retired from a hard life as a contractor in the 1970s, and began
to pass his idle time with whittling, carving and assembling of various lawn
ornaments. In a period of several years he made more than a dozen wind-
toys to place in his yard, with forms as diverse as ducks, animals and air-
planes. In his front yard he cut out and painted familiar storybook characters, while his garden was augmented with cutout painted flowers.

Ref: Flights of Fancy

REEVES, PHINEAS (1833-1896)
    Decoy carver   Port Rowan, Ontario
The Reeves name is well-known among decoy collectors, in that at least
Reeves carvers have been identified. Indeed there were three Reeves gen-
erations associated with the Long Point Duck Hunting Club. The master of
these carvers was Phineas, who made ducks and other birds for club
members in the 1870s. His finely carved ducks and Canada geese are among
the most coveted examples of decoy art.

Ref: Gates, Ontario Decoys

REID, DONALD (1862-1920)
    Decoy carver   Hamilton, Ontario
Although the Hamilton area is known for a group of carvers active in the
1930s and 1940s, an earlier figure of considerable importance was Don Reid.
He is known especially for distinctive hollow-body ducks with slender pro-
portions and graceful lines. Most are identifiable by the initials 'DR' branded
on the underside. Later carvers undoubtedly were influenced by the high
artistic merit of the Reid decoys.

Ref: Gates, Ontario Decoys

REIST, MOSES G. (active early 20th century)
    Calligrapher   Waterloo County, Ontario
Moses Reist was a member of the Old Order Mennonite community in the
Elmira area of Waterloo County. Early in life he was badly injured when a
horse kicked him in the head, and it was suggested that he had perhaps suf-
fered brain damage to the extent that from time to time he had to be

confined or hospitalized. During several of his periods of treatment at the Guelph Sanatorium, he lamented his forced separation from wife and friends, and would sometimes compose verses on paper or cardboard, some embellished with simple Pennsylvania German geometric motifs. He would sell his poetry for a dollar, as indicated at the top of each, the subject matter of which was a personal outpouring of his discouragement and frustration about the hardships of life in an asylum.

Ref: Bird and Kobayashi, A Splendid Harvest

RENTZ, EWALD (active 1970s and after)
    Woodcarver, sculptor   Beardmore, Ontario
Working at various jobs, this self-taught sculptor was at times a barber, and other times a prospector, having occasional success in finding gold in his travels in Northern Ontario. His attentive eye has benefitted his artistic interests as well, in that many of his creative sculptural undertakings are based upon unusual roots, fungus and other forms which he is able to find in the woods. He has talked frequently of his ability to find interesting forms 'in' the objects he picks up, bringing them to expression by small modifications of carving, painting or building-up with plastic wood. He thus has been able to make a turkey for remarkably little modification of the fungus-form from which it is derived. Other figures include a bellhop, ballet dancer, nativity scene, crucifixion and a variety of improbable characters. Many of his works are infused with humour or surprises, notably creatures having bodies of one species and heads of another.

Ref: Folk Art in Canada (catalogue); From the Heart
Coll: National Museum of Man (CCFCS)

REYNOLDS, CATHERINE (c. 1782-1864)
    Painter   Amherstburg, Ontario
Daughter of an English Commissary, she was born in Detroit, moving to Amherstburg after the British evacuation of Detroit. Her father built the fort on the Canadian side during the War of 1812. She did numerous amateur landscapes in pencil, crayon, sepia wash and watercolour of Essex County, Niagara Falls and Montréal, most dated between 1810-20.

Ref: Harper, Painters and Engravers; Harper, A People's Art;
Coll: Art Gallery of Ontario; Detroit Institute of Fine Arts; National Gallery of Canada

RHÉAUME, DAMASE (1832-1903)
    Woodcarver   Baie-Saint-Paul, Charlevoix County, Québec
A rather competent but self-taught woodcarver, this craftsman did bird and
animal carvings at his home on the north shore of the St. Lawrence River.
He is particularly known for a beautifully carved and painted small dove,   175
based less on religious imagery of this subject than on simple observation of
a bird as it exists in a natural setting.

Ref: Harper, *People's Art* (catalogue)

RICE, CYRIL (active 1970s and after)
    Yard artist   Bay Bulls Big Pond, near St. John's, Newfoundland
Cyril Rice has lived for many years at his small wooden cabin on the Southern Shore Highway near St. John's. In the summer months he brings out his
previously-made ornaments and carves or constructs yet other items for his
yard, combining plastic or other mass-produced objects with carved weathervanes, whirligigs and whimseys of his own making.

Ref: *Flights of Fancy*

RICHARD, DAMASE (1852-1922)
    Woodcarver   Portneuf County, Québec
An exceptionally refined, yet completely self-taught craftsman, Damase
Richard was a member of a family with numerous members talented in the
art of woodcarving. He produced in his lifetime many dozens of carved
birds, animals and other works in wood. In particular he carved several
finely-detailed hawks, owls, cats and various domestic animals.

Ref: Harper, *People's Art* (catalogue)
Coll: National Museum of Man (CCFCS)

RICHARDS, WILLIAM (c. 1784-1811)
    Painter   James Bay region
Born on the Albany River, Richard Williams was the child of a Welsh father
and Cree mother. He was raised by Cree people. Most of his life was spent in
the James Bay region, where he painted numerous views of fur-trading posts.
He had begun sketching before 1805, executing watercolour sketches of life
in the Moose Factory district. His is especially well-known for a watercolour

Riggs, Alfie (c. 1868-1940s). Satyr. Painted wood: early 20th century. Coll: New Brunswick Museum.

view, entitled A *South-east View of Albany Factory*, done c. 1805-10.

Ref: Harper, *People's Art* (catalogue); Public Archives of Canada
Coll: Hudson's Bay Company, Winnipeg

RIGGS, ALFRED (c. 1868- c. 1940s)
   Woodcarver   New Brunswick
For a considerable time referred to as 'Alfie the Whittler', the range and

quality of his work was not always recognized until recent years. He was born in the village of Fairfield, near St. Martin's, New Brunswick, and is believed to have spent some time in Halifax in his later years. It is believed that he died in England, where he had reportedly gained employment carving artificial limbs. His earliest known work is associated with a tale concerning an early effort to carve tiny harnesses for a large flock of pigeons supposedly intended to carry him aloft in a dubious aviation attempt (reportedly coming to a disastrous conclusion in the manure pile). He carved many animals and birds in his youth, and eventually carved a large and rather fine crucifix for St. Peter's Church in Portland. He is known also for carved heads, gargoyles, several relief plaques, a newel post and other works.

Ref: James, 'Sculptor or Whittler?'
Coll: New Brunswick Museum; Nova Scotia Museum

ROBERT, MADAME (active late 19th century)
    Rug maker   Saint-Jean-Baptiste de Rouville, Québec
Unfortunately, virtually nothing is known of the life of this exceptionally talented rug maker, but the hooked rug made by her in 1890 is surely one of the truly outstanding examples of textile folk art. It is a symmetrical arrangement of horses, fanciful animals of unclear definition, a tree of life, chalices, church spires and geometric decoration which indicates a highly imaginative mind and refinement of technical competence.

Ref: Folk Art in Canada (catalogue)
Coll: National Museum of Man (CCFCS), Nettie Sharpe Collection

ROBINSON, JONAS (1901-   )
    Painter   Merrickville, Ontario
Like many individuals who did not discover that they were endowed with artistic ability until late in life, Jonas Robinson began painting upon his retirement from an active farming career. His favourite subjects were those scenes which he could encounter on daily walks around his home. In particular, he was fond of rendering oil depictions of houses, businesses and familiar settings in the Merrickville area. His interest in the preservation of early buildings is reflected in the fact that he sometimes chose to depict vanishing landmarks, as in his 1980 painting of the Merrick woollen mill (built 1848, demolished 1979). His limitations as to proportion and perspectival accuracy are fre-

Rogerson, John (1837-after 1926). *Queen Victoria*. Painted and gilded wood: 1860s. Coll: New Brunswick Museum.

quently offset by strong colouration which give his paintings strong visual expressiveness.

Ref: National Museum of Man Archives (CCFCS)
Coll: National Museum of Man (CCFCS)

ROGERSON, JOHN (1837- c. 1920s)
     Woodcarver   Saint John, New Brunswick
Born at Lock Maben, Dumfrieshire, Scotland, John Rogerson arrived in Canada at the age of twelve. The young John was first exposed to the art of woodcarving when seeing carvings in the workshop of his uncle, Edward Charters, a master woodcarver and gilder by trade. John spent some time with Edward Charters as an apprentice, and then studied for two years with a woodcarver in Boston. John devoted several years to the carving of elaborate figureheads for ships, and the high quality of his workmanship was recognized on both sides of the Atlantic. When there was no longer a demand for this form of woodcarving, he was forced to seek other work, particularly as tide waiter in the local Customs House. He nevertheless continued to carve in his spare hours, producing several busts, some carving for local churches and an ornate chair for the St. Andrew's Society of Saint John. He is generally considered to be the master carver of Old Saint John.

Ref: James, 'The Last Woodcarver of Old Saint John'
Coll: New Brunswick Museum

ROTH, JACOB (1896-   )

Woodcarver, painter

new

Born in the Amish Mennonite community of southwestern Ontario, Jacob Roth possessed an immediate familiarity with the details of farm life. His interest in carving and painting was evident early in life. As a young man he injured himself in a fall from the barn roof, so that in later life he was to have trouble getting around. His earliest artistic activity dates from the 1930s. His many carvings depict varied aspects of farm life. He often combined painting with carving, as in the case of several ducks, or paintings with small cut-out birds placed on frames. Later he began to produce more complex works, notably horses pulling wagons. When any interest was shown in his work, he would busy himself, working for longer time periods to make elaborate tableaux. Among his favourite subjects are sugar-making scenes, gathering of Mennonites at the meeting house, dogs driving cattle home, auctions, horse races and barn-raising scenes. Many of the subjects are of a humorous nature, although one, entitled 'Circus Comes to Town', depicts an event which had been blamed for the outbreak of a cholera epidemic that had taken many lives in the Waterloo region. George Roth's versatile carving interests continued well into his eighties, when he produced some of his finest works.

Inf: John Harbinson

ROY, PHILIPPE (1899-1982)

Woodcarver   Saint-Philémon, Québec

There are probably few other known instances of a folk carver who so consistently produced inspired religious art as Philippe Roy. The connection between the gentle piety of his art and the spiritual humbleness of his life is extraordinarily strong. For most of his life he lived a somewhat secluded existence, staying in the home of his sister at Saint-Philémon. He first undertook carving in his 30s or 40s, reputedly small animals which he kept in his room and rarely showed to visitors. Among his first religious projects were a Nativity Scene which he carved for Christmas. It was only when he experienced several sieges of illness that he considered selling his work, gradually parting with some of his earlier carvings and then making Crèches upon request. His religious humility seems to be reflected in his art, particularly in

Roy, Phillippe (1899-1982). *Calvary*. Painted wood: 1978.

his biblical scenes, including the Flight into Egypt, The Fall and the
Crucifixion. With respect to his Crucifixion – or Calvary-carvings, he indicated that he was interested in the symbolism of each of the pieces, possibly
basing these on illustrations or wayside crosses. In one instance he explained
that he included the Serpent at the base of the Cross as the cause of the
Crucifixion, the presence of Joseph (rather than the customary John) in the
scene because of the importance of the idea of the Holy Family, and the
feature of a rooster upon a ball-in-cage to emphasize the notion of imprison-
ment as a consequence of the Fall of Man. There is a distinctive atmosphere
to these many Roy carvings, revealed especially in the profound serenity
characterizing the faces of each of the figures.

Ref: Harper, *People's Art* (catalogue); *From the Heart*
Coll: National Museum of Man (CCFCS)

ROY-AUDY, JEAN-BAPTISTE (1778- c. 1848)
Painter and cabinetmaker   Trois Rivières, Québec
A carpenter and cabinetmaker by trade, Roy-Audy was a self-taught painter
who later began to paint professionally in various cities of Québec, Ontario
and New York State. His earlier paintings are primarily of New Testament
scenes, done for churches, while in later years he worked increasingly as a
portrait artist. He did a portrait of a murderer which was auctioned off the
day after the hanging, giving it a somewhat unique place in history. His style
underwent changes, but he always retained a certain primitive hardness and
linear quality which serves to distinguish his work.

Ref: Harper, *Painters and Engravers*; Harper, A *People's Art*
Coll: Congregation of the Resurrection; Hôtel-Dieu, Québec; Musée du
    Québec; National Gallery of Canada

ROYS, SARAH MINERVA (active c. 1850)
Painter   Stormont County, Ontario
About this artist little is known, except for a quite exceptional theorem-
painting which she did while a pupil in eastern Ontario. As was the normal
practise in this art form, she painted an attractive vase of flowers by the use
of stencils for leaves and buds, employing a bright range of colours.

Ref: Harper, A *People's Art*
Coll: Upper Canada Village

RUSSELL, ARNOLD M. (1900-1976)
Painter   Prince Albert, Saskatchewan
Like many of his Saskatchewan counterparts, Arnold Russell was a retired
farmer who turned to painting in later years as a form of pleasure to occupy
his leisure hours. He did not restrict himself to merely historical or nostalgic
subjects, but rather based his various oil-on-masonite pictures upon a wide
range of subjects drawn from memory, fantasy or direct observation. This
diversity is suggested by titles such as 'The Cabin', '307' (a large steam-
locomotive), 'Prairie Harvest', 'The Homestead' and others. That his motive
may have been borne out of a sense of establishing continuity of the past
with the present is suggested by his daughter's claim that 'these meaningful
paintings were his way of preserving memories of the past'.

Ref: *Grassroots Saskatchewan; Seven Saskatchewan Folk Artists*
Coll: Saskatchewan Arts Board

Roys, Sarah Minerva (active 1850s). Theorem. Watercolour on paper:
c. 1850. Coll: Upper Canada Village.

ST-GERMAIN, ALCIDE (1911-   )
    Yard artist   St-Antonine-Abbé, Huntingdon County, Québec
His first carving was done on a modest scale in the form of small animals
which he kept in his room. Around the age of 50 he began to work out-
doors, making deer, giraffes, tigers birds and other pieces which he placed
on his lawn and in his garden. He soon began to make penguins, human
figures and other pieces which seemed to be humourous comments of one
form or another, and to make carved groupings for the exterior of his
house and yard.

Ref: les patenteux du Québec

SAUVE, ARTHUR (1896-1973)
    Woodcarver   Maxwell, Ontario
An amateur whittler and carver, he made a considerable range of whirligigs,

crucifixions, musical instruments and carved human figures, ranging from rather coarse chip-carved works to comparatively competent sculptural forms.

Ref: McKendry, *Folk Art*

SAVOIE, AMATEUR (1896-   )
    Decoy carver, woodcarver   Neguac, New Brunswick
Possibly the best-known of New Brunswick decoy makers, Amateur 'Mat' Savoie was a barber (self-taught), cobbler and folk artist at Neguac. His carving output between 1905 and the late 1960s was prolific. It is estimated that he produced in excess of 5,000 decoys and decorative birds. In addition, he is known for model boats, sleighs, miniature carved animals and decorated crooked knives. After 1940 he began to devote more attention to refinement of what had earlier been somewhat rough-cut decoys. He made many geese and blackducks for sale to local hunters, and became so well-known for his carving ability that other hunters began to pay him to fashion wooden heads which they could attach to their own decoy bodies. Much of his later work is not only signed and dated but also features the unusual inscription of the temperature of the day on which it was made.

Ref: Guyette and Guyette, *Decoys of Maritime Canada*

SAWLER, STAN (1877-1966)
    Decoy carver   Western Shore, Nova Scotia
A contemporary of Percy Shupe and neighbour in the small village of Western Shore, Stan Sawler was a guide and dory builder. His mergansers are remarkable for their sleek, elongated contours. Like Percy Shupe, he used combs cut from leather.

Ref: Steve and Linda Kangas, *Decoys: A North American Survey*

SCALON, THOMAS (c. 1880-1970)
    Model maker   Rockwood, Ontario
Raised on a farm in Eramosa Township, Wellington County, he was an itinerant clock and watch repairer at Rockwood. He made models, including a rocking boat (a model ship) for his nephew, who by the time of its completion was too old to be interested in it. Nevertheless this

Schweitzer, Rebecca (active 1880s). Hooked rug. Wool on burlap: 1886.

finely-constructed ship was set aside and admired for many years.

Ref: National Museum of Man Archives (CCFCS)
Coll: National Museum of Man (CCFCS)

SCHNEIDERMAN, GOLDYE (active 1960s and after)
   Painter   Montréal, Québec
Also known as 'Grandma Goldye', she began to paint late in life, taking up
art as a pastime around 1967. Her canvases are often deliberately whimsical
or fanciful, featuring unusual seascapes, landscapes, still-life scenes, portraits,
nudes or anecdotal subjects.

Ref: National Museum of Man Archives (CCFCS)
Coll: National Museum of Man (CCFCS)

SCHULER, HENRY (active 1867-1880s)
   Potter   Paris and Brantford, Ontario
Born in Illinois in 1842, Henry Schuler moved to Canada, operating
earthenware potteries at New Hamburg and Paris, and then stoneware firms
at Paris and Brantford. He produced blue-decorated stoneware with floral
designs, and in 1878 showed his wares at the Paris (France) Universal Exhibition.

Ref: Newlands, Early Ontario Potters

SCHWEITZER, REBECCA (active late 19th century)
   Rug maker   New Hamburg, Ontario
Numerous rug-makers of Waterloo county produced hooked mats when
patterns and growing interest led to a widespread practise of the hobby in
the 1880s and 1890s. Rebecca Schweitzer was a part of this phenomenon, but
is somewhat unusual in that her rugs reflect aspects of her Continental-
Germanic decorative background, rather than the standardized designs
popular in North America. She made many rugs, but the outstanding
achievement was an extraordinary large example featuring two uniformed
soldiers with swords facing each other in a standing position. This motif
appears elsewhere in heraldry and in rare instances of Pennsylvania fraktur
and painted furniture, but its incorporation within the decorative format of
a hooked rug is highly exceptional.

Ref: Bird and Kobayashi, A Splendid Harvest

SCOMOROCO, CATHERINE (active early 20th century)
Rug maker   Kitchener, Ontario
Catherine Scomoroco was a member of the Polish community in Kitchener,
with many relatives living in the Wilno area of Renfrew County. In her later
years she made more than a dozen highly refined and decorative hooked
rugs, some with flowers, others with lions, peacocks and whimsical animals.
She had made rugs for every room of her house on Strange Street in
Kitchener, each with an extraordinarily distinctive design and
colour scheme.

Ref: Bird, Canadian Folk Art

SEAMAN, ABRAHAM (1767-1848)
Gravestone carver   Horton-Cornwallis area, Nova Scotia
Descended from New York Loyalists, Abraham Seaman made numerous
stones in the Horton-Cornwallis district, featuring distinctively carved angel
heads, crossed branches and other motifs. On the basis of known gravemarkers, it would appear that he was active during the approximate period of
1812-1821.

Ref: Trask, Life How Short

'SECOND HORTON CARVER', (active 1798-1805)
Gravestone carver   Kings County, Nova Scotia
There is evidence of a stonecutter (possibly two) working in the Horton-
Cornwallis district, whose work is recognized by sad cherubim-motifs, rope
carving and distinctive border design.

Ref: Trask, Life How Short

SHANTZ BROTHERS (c. 1924-1940s)
Whittlers   Woolwich Township, Waterloo County, Ontario
Four Shantz brothers were active woodcarvers near St. Jacobs in Waterloo
County, making chip-carved shelves, wallboxes, picture frames and toys for
nearly two decades. Each of these brothers (Levi, Elam, Erwin, Orvie) carved
a hanging shelf with geometric, horseshoe and floral motifs, some painted in
strong colours. Orvie Shantz was also an amateur painter, and made a charming watercolour picture of the Shantz home at Lexington. Undoubtedly
some of the techniques used were learned when the boys were pupils at the

Silver, Francis (1841-1920). *The Hantsport.* Painted wood: late 19th century.
Coll: Hantsport Memorial Community Centre

Lexington School, but there is also evidence of influence from the well-known transient woodcarver Fred G. Hoffman (see entry) who stayed in many Mennonite homes in the area.

Ref: Bird and Kobayashi, A *Splendid Harvest*

SHINK, JOSEPH (1884-1913)
   Woodcarver   Beaumont, Québec
Descended from a line of Germanic settlers who had migrated earlier from Europe to Québec, Joseph Shink was known early in the 20th century for his hobby of carving in this village east of Québec City. He carved birds and animals of various kinds, but is particularly well-known for his human figures. He made some religious figures, and a broad range of carvings of farmers and villagers engaged in domestic activities.

Ref: arts populaires catalogue Lessard, *L'art traditionnel au Québec*
Coll: Musée du Québec

SILVER, FRANCIS (1841-1920)

Painter   Hantsport, Nova Scotia
Born in Portugal, Francis da Silva (later re-named Silver) emigrated to
Hantsport, Nova Scotia in 1861. He was married in 1865 to Elizabeth Arnold.
His early years involved sea travel and the raising of his family. He eventually
took employment with E. Churchill and Sons, where he did gardening and
maintenance of the large Churchill estate. He was a member of the
Hantsport Baptist Church, and his religious interests were on several occasions expressed in his paintings. In Winter hours he did painting in the basement, using the walls, sailcloth and wooden panels. Later he used the Carriage House for his expanding artistic interests, painting scenes of the harbour, historical topics, seafaring themes and even political cartoons with captions, depicting an innocent agrarian Canada being seduced by a worldly-
wise industrial United States.

Ref: Art Gallery of Nova Scotia, *Francis Silver*
Coll: Hantsport Memorial Community Centre; Public Archives of Nova Scotia

SINCLAIR, IRVING (active early 20th century)

    Painter   New Westminster, British Columbia
Irving Sinclair was a self-taught painter who depicted marine subjects in both
oil and watercolour. He is known to have produced numerous pictures of
shipping along lower British Columbia, including a painting of the ship
'Beaver' in 1910. One of his most unusual endeavours was a picture of a ship
at sea which he painted on the tail of a baby whale cast ashore on Galliano Island.

Coll: New Westminster Museum

SHUPE, PERCY (1877-1962)

    Decoy carver   Western Shore, Nova Scotia
A productive carver, Percy Shupe made many solid decoys. He is known to
have carved as many as a hundred sets of mergansers, each with one drake
and three hens. The drakes are distinguished by slender heads and combs
made of leather.

Ref: Kangas and Kangas, *Decoys: A North American Survey*

SIMARD, JOSEPH-ÉLIE (1917-   )
    Yard artist   Grande-Baie, Dubuc County, Québec
Joseph-Élie Simard had for many years worked with wood, but after the
mid-1950s began to give his work a more public place, moving various carved
objects from his workroom to his front lawn. In addition to many carved
birds and animals, he made several free-standing large human figures as well
as relief plaques depicting pigs feeding and other familiar farm scenes. Much
of his interest was drawn not only from observation of local detail, but also
from reading, including a number of mythological figures which he placed
along the front of his house.

Ref: les patenteux du Queébec

SIMCOE, MRS. JOHN GRAVES (1766-1850)
    Painter, sketch artist   Upper Canada
Elizabeth, wife of Lieutenant Governor John Graves Simcoe, accompanied
her husband to Canada in 1791, and produced a number of amateur works
during her stay from 1791-1796. She made many sketches of historical and
topographical interest.

Ref: Harper, Painters and Engravers; Heritage of Brant
Coll: British Museum; Ontario Archives; Public Archives of Canada

SKERRY, GEORGE (1916-1965)
    Decoy carver   Malpeque Bay, Prince Edward Island
The skill of decoy carving seems to have come easily and early to George
Skerry. He was actively involved in making decoys when still a teen-aged
boy living at Lot 16, selling many models to resident hunters and visitors
along the entire Malpeque Bay shoreline. A carpenter and boatbuilder,
Skerry divided his leisure time between fishing and decoy making. His output of geese, brant, blackduck, teal, plover and curlew decoys is estimated
at several hundred. Most were rootheads, with visible whittling marks as dis-
tinguishing features.

Ref: Guyette and Guyette, Decoys of Maritime Canada

SKINNER, SAMUEL (active 1849-1864)
    Potter   Picton, Ontario
An American craftsman who joined the migration to Canada of the first half

Sleep, Joseph (1914-1978). *Sailing Ship*. Ink and pencil on paper: 1973. Coll: National Museum of Man (CCFCS).

of the 19th century, he joined with William Hart in the making of decorated stoneware at the newly-established pottery at Picton, in Prince Edward County. The Skinner-Hart period produced many finely decorated examples with flowers, birds and tree motifs in cobalt blue colour.

Ref: Newlands, *Early Ontario Potters*; Webster, *Early Canadian Pottery*
Coll: Royal Ontario Museum (Sigmund Samuel Canadiana Collection)

SLEEP, JOSEPH (1914-1978)
    Painter   Halifax, Nova Scotia
Born on a boat 'somewhere between England and Canada', Joseph, or Joe, Sleep grew up in Saint John, New Brunswick, attending school for only a few years. He later worked at miscellaneous jobs in the Maritimes and Ontario, and in 1930, by his own report, worked for five dollars a month for MacKenzie King. From 1949-1970 he was jack-of-all-trades for the Bill Lynch Shows, a travelling circus which toured many cities and towns in the Atlantic Provinces. He was interned in 1973 at the Halifax Infirmary, where nurses and

other staff provided him paper and supplies so that he began to draw posters for them. 'I started drawing my own and I ain't stopped since', he said shortly before his death (*Joe Sleep Retrospective*, p.26). In the 1970s he began to display his work at his studio at 1671 Argyle Street, Halifax, advertising his paintings of fish and ships, 'in all sizes, on masonite and bristolboard, as well as hand crafted models of ships and trawlers, all for sale at very reasonable prices'. Without pension or other sources of income, painting was Joe Sleep's sole means of financial support in his later years. Using subject matter drawn sometimes from observation, other times from his vivid imagination, mass media or memories of his circus days, Joe Sleep painted not merely for himself but also for his public. He used many materials – latex, felt markers, pen, pencil, ballpoint and even spray paint – on paper, cardboard, canvas and masonite. His technique was in part governed by the need to produce work in significant quantity, hence the use of hand-made cardboard stencils of animals and other images which could be arranged in an endless variety of compositions, each given further decorative embellishments. In addition to his well-known cats, Joe Sleep also drew fish, domestic and exotic animals, trees, birds, boats and other images. His works are generally comprised of heavily concentrated arrays of animals and surrounding motifs enclosed within floral or geometric borders drawn and painted in vibrant colours. Some paintings are of 'suitcase size', easily packed and taken away by tourists who might purchase them when visiting Halifax, while others are monumental compositions painted on panels eight feet in length.

Ref: Folk Art of Nova Scotia; From the Heart; Joe Sleep Retrospective
Coll: Art Gallery of Nova Scotia; National Museum of Man (CCFCS)

SMITH, ABIGAIL (active 1860s)
    Rug maker   New Maryland, New Brunswick
A craftswoman living at this small village near Fredericton, she is believed to be the maker of what may very well be the earliest known dated and signed Canadian hooked rug.

Ref: Ramsay Traquair, 'Hooked Rugs in Canada'
Coll: New Brunswick Museum

SMITH, BRUCE (c. 1915-   )
    Woodcarver   Bethany, Ontario
He worked for many years at General Electric in Peterborough, and upon

Smith, Abigail (active 1860s). Hooked rug. Wool on burlap: 1860. Coll: New Brunswick Museum.

retirement found time for his hobbies of bee-keeping, gardening and wood-carving. He began by carving birds, pigs, horses, dogs and various models of wagons, animals and people. His carved figures are generally given a high shellac or varnish coating. In later years he carved some religious subjects, notably a crucifix and the Good Shepherd. When considering the possibility of selling his work, he was inclined to place high prices on his carvings, using as a guideline his experience at General Electric where cost is determined in relation to hourly labour. He would often go long periods without carving, then become active when prodded by those appreciative of his work, inspiring the observation of one collector that 'sometimes even folk artists need a public'.

Inf: Ralph and Patricia Price
Coll: National Museum of Man (CCFCS)

SMITH, RANDALL (1906-   )
    Woodcarver   Ingomar, Shelburne Co., Nova Scotia
Randall grew up in a fishing community and naturally followed the sea, travelling widely both North and South. He later worked as a carpenter and

took to carving around 1970 at first making large codfish and shark weathervanes. Fish have been his specialty, but he has made boats, butterflies, a large
dragonfly and painted faces on smooth flat rocks.

Inf: Chris Huntington

SNOW, LEONARD
Yard artist   Carbonear, Conception Bay, Newfoundland
The house and lawn of Leonard and Myrtle Snow were transformed in
dramatic manner after the 1960s by a combination of carving, assembly and
painting. The yard was enclosed within a board fence painted red, blue and
white, a colour scheme to be echoed again and again on the house, shed,
posts and objects in the lawn. He cut out swans, roosters and other forms
from plywood, placing these on the roof and atop poles, constructed whirligigs from wood and plastic jugs, made various kinds of weathervanes and
used found materials such as plastic horses and real moose antlers for
decoration of both yard and buildings.

Ref: *Flights of Fancy*

SNOWIE, ALLAN (1922-   )
Woodcarver   Edmonton, Alberta
Born in Melrose, Scotland, Allan Snowie came to Canada in 1957. His extensive woodworking skills were to serve him well in Edmonton, where he
became an instructor of carpentry for Alberta Workmen's Compensation.
He had long enjoyed making articles of wood for family and self-amusement.
As a young man he made toys for his children. In later life he turned to the
carving of birds and various figures. One of his most elaborate undertakings
was a full-scale rally bicycle, made entirely of wood, for which he received
an award in 1983.

Inf: Allan Snowie

SOLOMON (active 1844)
Painter   Québec
Very little information is available concerning the life of this artist. He is
known for a spirited oil landscape view of *Saint Andrews, Québec From Abbott's
Hill*, reputedly completed at the house built by the father of Sir John
Abbott (1821-1893), Canada's first native-born Prime Minister. The painting

Somerville, Dan (active mid-19th century). Chairs. Painted and stained wood: 1852.

uses the cliche conventions of 18th-century French landscapes, but is naive in perspective and charming in its strong colours.

Ref: Harper, *People's Art* (catalogue)
Coll: Historical Society of Argenteuil County

SOMERVILLE, DAN (active mid-19th century)
   Woodcarver   St-Hillaire, Québec
He is known as the carver of a pair of extraordinary rustic chairs (lady's and gentlemen's) with arms, back and legs made of tree branches and roots. The

chairs are remarkable in their features with male and female heads carved on the chair backs. Elsewhere there are carved masks, snakes and various decorative features. The chairs are signed and dated 1852.

Ref: Waddington's catalogue (June 21-22, 1982)   195

SOOS, TONY

new Woodcarver   Halifax, Nova Scotia; Dorchester, New Brunswick
Mr. Soos was a Hungarian refugee who spent a number of years as a prisoner at Dorchester Penitentiary where he made a number of 10-16″ carvings, painted and unpainted, of Hungarian cavalry officers mounted, soldiers and angels holding lamps. He also made several six-foot models of Hungarian galleons.

Inf: Chris Huntington

SPENCER, SAM A. (1898-   )
   Carver and painter   Saskatoon, Saskatchewan
Born in England, Sam Spencer came to Saskatchewan as an orphan. By his own account, he started carving in 1927, his first projects being hand-made picture frames. One of his earliest efforts was a frame to hold an old calendar which his grandmother hesitated to throw out. The frame made it possible to keep the calendar without having to worry about its destruction. A prolific craftsman, he carved perhaps close to a hundred works in his life-time, using few tools other than a jack-knife and a pocket-knife. His talent was a double one, allowing him to work both at carving and painting. Many of his pictures are taken from popular sources, including photographs, calendars and illustrated children's books. His earlier works were often in the form of decorated functional items, including frames, wall-racks and shelves. Subjects included horses, birds and various animals, while scenes ranged from hunting, military parades, Indian war dances, hockey games and scenes from childhood to portraits and a Last Supper.

Ref: From the Heart; Grassroots Saskatchewan; Prairie Folk Art
Coll: National Museum of Man (CCFCS)

STEADMAN, GEORGE (1910-   )
   Sculptor   Oshawa, Ontario
George Steadman's artistic flowering came late in life. He had always

Spencer, Sam A. (1898-   ). *Angel and Child*. Painted wood: 1965. Coll:
National Museum of Man (CCFCS).

managed to find spare time from his work at General Motors to assemble
imaginative structures from wood, metal and discarded articles. Upon his
retirement, he immersed himself fully in his pastime. In his use of found
materials, he is a 'junk sculptor' in the tradition of such figures as the English
artist Rowland Emett. Indeed, one of Steadman's creations, *The Afternoon Tea
Train to Walden Spinney*, is attributed to Emett. His first inspiration came from

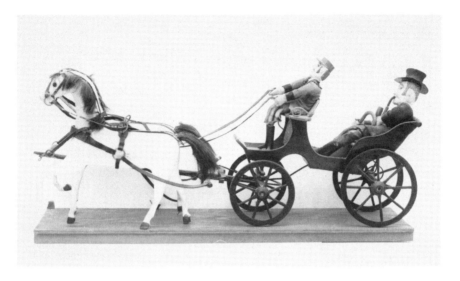

Stefanchuk, William (active mid-20th century). *The Outing*. Painted wood and plaster: c. 1950.

Jack Didion, a senior artist and designer at General Motors, who introduced Steadman to the technique of brazing various metals together. Using gears, tin cans, old locks, chains, buttons or any other objects of interest, George Steadman managed to construct trains and other subjects which are refreshing, imaginative and humorous.

Inf: Joan Murray
Ref: Good Heavens

STEFANCHUK, WILLIAM (active mid-20th century)
   Woodcarver   Tolstoi, Manitoba
During his childhood in the Ukraine William Stefanchuk was trained to be a carriage maker. After emigrating to Canada in the 1930s, he worked at farming and various jobs in Manitoba. When he turned his energies to an active hobby of woodcarving, he found that vocation and avocation were not far apart. In the 1950s and 1960s he constructed numerous miniature carts and carriages, reminiscent of the functional large counterparts he had made earlier. Many of his works take the form of tableaux, depicting aspects of farm or small-town life. In one instance, he shows himself as a hard-working farmer behind an ox-drawn plow, while in another case he shows the pom-

pous village gentry off on a Sunday outing, making a proud display of himself, his fancy buggy and galloping horses.

Inf: Michael Rowan
Ref: From the Heart
Coll: National Museum of Man (CCFCS)

STILES, G. (c. 1899-   )
    Woodcarver   Riverside, New Brunswick
A retired farmer whose artistic interests are strongly grounded in his agrarian experiences, he carved and constructed various models at his home near Moncton. Most of his constructions involved farm vehicles with hand-carved drivers and other human figures. His carvings of horses, oxen and other animals are primitive in execution.

Ref: 'Twas Ever Thus
Coll: National Museum of Man (CCFCS)

STONE, NATHAN (active 1970s and after)
    Yard artist   Bryant's Cove, Conception Bay, Newfoundland
Having worked at a wide variety of jobs, mostly part-time, throughout his life, Nathan Stone retired on a full-time basis in the early 1970s and began to decorate his 85 year old house at Bryant's Cove. His techniques involved whittling, constructing and sometimes simply arranging of found objects. Among his projects are painted wooden boat models, a carved propeller-driven airplane, a church, railway cars (which he named 'Newfie Bullets'), other vehicles and animals.

Ref: Flights of Fancy

STRYJEK, DMYTRO (1899-   )
    Painter   Hafford, Saskatchewan
Within the Ukrainian communities of western Canada there are often to be found many extraordinarily capable craftspersons who draw upon techniques and subject-matter rooted in their European background. One of these is the self-taught painter Dmytro Stryjek, born at Lanivtski in the southwest Ukraine in 1899. Upon the arrival of the family in 1923, Dmytro took on various odd jobs in and around Hafford, eventually gaining employment with a Canadian National Railway section crew. He worked at this job

Stryjek, Dmytro (1899-   ). *Archbishop Metropolitan Sheptycky*. Enamels, ball-point and pencil on card: c. 1979.

for many years. For most of his life he resided within the close-knit Ukrainian community at Hafford and in the Saskatoon area. Although he may always have expressed some degree of interest in drawing, it was not until the 1950s that he began to use spare hours in the evenings to do small drawings, especially tiny portraits on 3" X 5" cards. His artist's tools were pencil and ball-point pen. Many of his first drawings were of neighbours in Hafford. He gradually broadened his subject matter to include Ukrainian heroes, contemporary political figures and public celebrities whose pictures appeared in magazines and newspapers. The occasion of his retirement in 1965 provided Dmytro with the opportunity to give fuller attention to his artistic pursuit. He now found himself spending time at the photographic studio operated by his son at Humboldt, where the many photographic portraits on display or in the process of being printed for customers provided further inspiration for drawn and painted depictions of human figures. In 1967 he moved to an apartment in Saskatoon and undertook an increasingly varied range of themes, including landscapes, buildings and local personalities. In particular he painted pictures of contemporary figures appearing in the media, notably Queen Elizabeth, Gabrielle Roy, Indira Ghandhi, Roy McMurtry, Pierre Trudeau and various popular entertainers. Many of the paintings from this period depict personal recollections or well-known stories of Ukrainian life. Working on paper and card, he used many materials to achieve what he considered a realistic approach, as for example in his inclusion of actual facial makeup to approximate natural colouring in his later portraits. His sources were many – imagination, memory, and the mass media whose visual expression he adapted freely to his own purposes.

Inf: Peter Millard
Ref: Mendel Art Gallery, *Dmytro Stryjek*; Millard, 'Dmytro Strykek: Innovative Folk Painting'
Coll: Mendel Art Gallery; Saskatchewan Arts Board; Susan Whitney Gallery

SUTTLE, CHARLIE (1914-   )
    Woodcarver   Lockeport, Shelburne County, Nova Scotia
Born in England, Charlie came to Canada in 1940 as a carpenter with the British Technical Mission. He was at times active as a sculptor, making figures of many kinds. His shop 'Joe's Lunch' in Lockeport featured his own abstract 'Mexican' painted decoration, as well as a large sign in the form of a haddock which he carved and painted for the business. His work includes human figures, fish, spiders and even religious subjects with a modernistic bent.

Ref: *Folk Art of Nova Scotia*; Waddington's catalogue (June 15-17, 1980)

SWEETMAN, HARRIET (active 1830s)
    Painter   Prince Edward County, Ontario
Little is known of the life of this amateur artist. She is the painter who produced several watercolour landscapes, and drawings in pencil and chalk. Par-

FLOCK OF IMPORTED COTSWOLD SHEEP. PROPERTY OF LAIDLAW & JACKSON WILTON GROVE

Swift, Joseph (d. 1889). *Flock of Imported Cotswold Sheep*. Watercolour on paper: 1887. Coll: Royal Ontario Museum.

ticularly well-known are several views of Prince Edward County and scenes along the Lake Ontario waterfront.

Ref: Harper, A *People's Art*

SWIFT, JOSEPH (-1889)

Painter   Toronto, Ontario

Possibly either James or a Joseph Swift who advertised his studio at 40 Euclid Avenue in Toronto, he is known on the basis of perhaps a dozen or more exceptional watercolour and oil paintings. His subjects are, almost without exception, of various domestic animals which farmers took to the annual Toronto Exhibition, forerunner of the Canadian National Exhibition. Most of his paintings are, then, animal portraits, inscribed with names of proud owners and notices of awards won. It is likely that Swift set up a temporary studio each year on the Exhibition grounds, painting upon request of prize winning owners. Works such as his well-known 'Flock of Imported Cotswold Sheep' (1887) are especially charming and outstanding naive paintings.

Ref: Harper, A *People's Art*
Coll: Royal Ontario Museum (Sigmund Samuel Canadiana Collection)

Thomarat, Jeanne A. (1893-   ). *Le Beaujolais.* Oil on canvas: 1976. Coll: National Museum of Man (CCFCS).

TANNER, CHARLIE (1904-1982)
Woodcarver   Eagle's Head, Nova Scotia
A fisherman at Eagle's Head in Queens County, he later found occasion to indulge his interest in woodcarving. Following his retirement in 1973, he dedicated several hours a day to his hobby. He made decoys, sailboats and various carved animals and human figures. At first he carved pieces for his own enjoyment, but soon began to sell them to visitors.

Ref: Charlie Tanner Retrospective (Art Gallery of Nova Scotia, 1984);
Folk Art of Nova Scotia

TAYLOR, GEORGE (active c. 1880-1918)
Potter   Port Hope, Ontario
Succeeding his father, James Taylor, George operated an earthenware pottery at Port Hope until the business closed in 1918. He is known for a

number of highly ornate covered jars, whose applied decorative elements include profusions of vines and flowers.

Ref: Newlands, *Early Ontario Potters;*
Coll: Royal Ontario Museum (Sigmund Samuel Canadiana Collection)   203

THOMARAT, JEANNE (1893-   )
    Painter   Duck Lake, Saskatchewan
Jeanne Thomarat's family left France when she was fourteen years old, migrating to what at the time was a forbiddingly remote and undeveloped destination in western Canada. Jeanne may have long sensed that she possessed painting abilities, and her understanding of design problems is undoubtedly rooted in her early training as a pattern maker. It appears that she did not commence painting before 1952. Her artistic motivation would seem to be coloured by a pervasive nostalgia for her beloved European homeland. Through her artistic powers, she could perhaps capture in painting what she could no longer hope to obtain in reality – a return to her fondly remembered home. In her own words, 'I thought I'd never get back to France and I wished to paint the places I love, the places I'll never see again' ('Prairie Folk Art', *artscanada*, 1979). She is the epitome of the 'memory painter', expressing through her oil paintings a charming, perhaps romanticized recollection of the bright orchards, flowers, trees, gardens and places of a happy youth. These are idyllic scenes of undisturbed tranquillity, pictures of childhood innocence, sadly removed by the vastness of geographical and chronological distance.

Ref: From the Heart; 'Prairie Folk Art' (*artscanada*, 1979)
Coll: National Museum of Man (CCFCS)

THORNBECK, GLORIA (active 1960s)
    Painter   Tyrone, Ontario
A self-taught artist, she recorded scenes of village life in and around Tyrone. Some of her pictures are observations of contemporary events, while others are probably derived from earlier photographs or illustrations, as, for example, her oil-on-masonite painting of Tyrone Mill with the busy traffic of people and vehicles in the foreground.

Ref: 'Twas Ever Thus
Coll: National Museum of Man (CCFCS)

Thorne, Joseph Bradshaw (1869-1963). *The Ancient Briton.* Oil on canvas: 1961.

THORNBECK, GLORIA (active mid-20th century and after)
    Painter   Tyrone, Ontario
This self-taught painter was a recorder of local places, some of which were in process of change or destruction. In the early 1960s she produced an oil painting on masonite of the old mill at Tyrone, surrounded by the activity of workers and children passing by on their way to play.

Ref: 'Twas Ever Thus

THORNE, JOSEPH BRADSHAW (1869-1963)
    Painter   Toronto, Ontario
In the description of his great-grandson, Joseph Bradshaw Thorne was born in working-class England and died in working-class Toronto. He was born in Wellingborough, Northamptonshire, north of London. He left school at age 13, the minimum allowable age, and took his first job, at Keen's Mustard Factory. His steadiest employment was with Chubb's Safe Works, installing vaults in banks. In his spare time he indulged his love of cricket, boating, fishing, running, marbles and music. In 1905, following an altercation with a new foreman at Chubb's and after six months of unemployment, he emigrated to Canada, obtaining work briefly on a farm near Goderich before settling on land in Toronto later in the year. He held many odd jobs, digging wells, making fence posts, working at a munitions factory. His artistic interests took the form of writing homely poetry and beginning to paint recollections of the old days in England and of events in Toronto. His various oil paintings, done in vibrant colours, depict English pubs, the 'Great Eastern' ship on which his father-in-law had worked as a construction man, and several self-portraits. He also painted famous sportsmen in the fields of rowing and marbles, a strong man who could lift a horse, a 700-pound man and other unusual characters. He painted portraits of several friends, the Davenport Station when it was demolished in the early 1930s and other works. Many of his paintings were humorous in nature, further accented by captions. His last self-portrait was painted at the age of ninety-two years.

Ref: Cummings, The Group of One: Joseph Bradshaw Thorne; Kobayashi et al, Folk
    Treasures of Ontario

THRESHER, G. (active mid-19th century)
    Painter   Maritime Canada
Little is known of the life of this artist, but he is represented by several

Tompkins, J. Seton (1899-   ). *Adam and Eve.* Painted wood: 1982.

paintings done c. 1850 of Halifax Harbour and Charlottetown Harbour.

Ref: National Museum of Man Archives (Thomas Lackey file) (CCFCS)

TIEDEMANN, H.O. (1821-1891)
    Painter, architect   Victoria, British Columbia
A topographical artist and architect, he emigrated to Canada in 1858, travel-
ing immediately to British Columbia. He visited Cariboo in 1862 and accompanied exploration parties into the interior in 1872. He designed the first
British Columbia Parliament Buildings in 1859, and other structures, including
lighthouses and the courthouse in 1888. Only in a marginal sense can his
work be called naive, suggested in a few exceptional watercolour pictures
done on surveying expeditions.

Ref: Harper, A *People's Art*
Coll: Provincial Archives of British Columbia

TODD, ROBERT CLOW (1809-1866)
    Painter   Québec City area, Québec
Born in England, Todd emigrated to Canada in 1834. He commenced business
in Québec City as a 'house, carriage and ornamental painter'. He lived briefly
on a farm at Montmorency where, it is reputed, Indians were allowed to
sleep in his kitchen. He moved to Toronto around 1854, remaining there
until at least 1865. His paintings tend to emphasize leisure pursuits, as in depictions of gentry and families on sleigh rides against the Montmorency Falls
background. Many of these works may have been commissioned, and exhibit a strong linear quality reminiscent of contemporary prints or lithographs
from which their style may be derived.

Ref: Harper, *Painter and Engravers*; Harper, A *People's Art*
Coll: National Gallery of Canada

TOMPKINS, J. SETON (1899-   )
    Woodcarver   Singhampton, Ontario
He worked at many odd jobs in this village south of Collingwood, including
a long period as the owner of an automobile repair business. In later years
he began to devote increased time to the woodworking hobby which had
always dominated his spare moments. His carved subjects are many and
diverse, including various animals depicted singly or in group situations. In

Trask, Fred (1946-   ). *Prison Cafeteria.* Acrylic on canvas: 1975.

particular he created many groupings in which dramatic impact was conveyed by a confrontation-situation, as in a cat staring up at a bird, a dog treeing a squirrel, or a matador provoking a bull. Other moments of tension are registered in the portrayal of a circus trainer coaxing a horse to stand on its hind legs. He also carved several religious scenes, including the Fall and the Crucifixion.

Ref: From the Heart; Kobayashi et al, *Folk Treasures of Historic Ontario;* 'Twas Ever Thus
Coll: National Museum of Man (CCFCS)

TRASK, FRED (1946-   )
    Painter   Halifax, Nova Scotia
He was born at Digby and lived in his younger years in an apartment above
his father's barbershop. He described himself as a 'hell-raiser' in his youth.
Echoing his own comments about wishing to re-live his childhood years, his
paintings have a child-like simplicity. He did painting in the 1970s and after,
using acrylic on various materials. Depicting a variety of daily events, his pictures show people eating in a cafeteria or going out for a Sunday ride in a
summer wagon. Like the work of children, his pictures tend to ignore
natural perspective and simply place walls and objects at parallel positions to
the four sides of the composition.

Ref: Folk Art of Nova Scotia; Waddington's catalogue (June 21-22, 1982)
Coll: Art Gallery of Nova Scotia; National Museum of Man (CCFCS)

TREMBLAY, MRS. D. (active c. 1878)
    Painter   New Brunswick
Little is known of this amateur artist's life, but her spirited style is evidenced
in a signed oil painting of a ship tragedy, done as a memorial to a sailor lost
at sea when his ship, the Anglo-Saxon, was wrecked in 1878.

Ref: Harper, People's Art (catalogue)

TRUDEAU, ANGUS (c. 1910-1984)
    Woodcarver, painter Wikemikong Reserve, Manitoulin Island, Ontario
An Odawa Indian, Angus Trudeau did various boat models and paintings of
lake boats which travelled around the Manitoulin Island area of Lake Huron.
Eventually his works were to be seen by a wider public after being shown at
a Toronto gallery.

Ref: National Museum of Man Archives (Thomas Lackey file) (CCFCS)
Coll: Department of Northern and Indian Affairs (Ontario)

TRUDEL, OVIDE (1909-   )
    Woodcarver   St-Prosper, Champlain County, Québec
Late in life he devoted spare time and especially the days of his retirement
to enjoying a whittling and carving hobby. He made numerous miniature
looms, working in the manner of actual ones, as well as

Trudeau, Angus (c. 1910-1984). *Manitou: Georgian Bay*. Acrylic on canvas: c. 1960. Coll: Indian and Northern Affairs.

tiny houses, stoves and farm vehicles pulled by hand-carved horses.

Ref: les patenteux de Québec

TULLY, BUD (1918-1973)

Decoy carver   Peterborough, Ontario

At first using decoys made by the Peterborough Canoe Company, Bud Tully began in his mid-20s to carve his own birds. Eventually he became increasingly busy with orders to make decoys for other hunters in the Peterborough area. Characteristically, he made solid-body ducks, with two large holes drilled in the bottom. Tully decoys generally exhibit highly competent carving and painting.

Ref: Gates, Ontario Decoys

TURGEON, ADÉLARD (1883-1969)

Woodcarver   Saint Anseline, Québec

In his retirement years at this tiny village in Dorchester County he found opportunity to apply his energies to the making of various pieces for each of his sisters. His works include a carved tree, human figures and animals. He was especially fond of carving musicians and characters engaged in everyday scenes of village life. He made numerous toys, miniature farm buildings, and carved a crucifix with Christ-figure.

Ref: 'Folk Art in Canada' (catalogue)
Coll: National Museum of Man (CCFCS

TURNER, ERNEST HARLAND (1871-1950)
Woodcarver   New Ross, Nova Scotia
Ernest Turner was a prospector who discovered a magnesium and a tin mine near this small Lunenburg County village. Throughout life he carved, often from found natural materials, such as roots. He made many species of birds and animals for friends, relatives and visitors.

Ref: Folk Art of Nova Scotia

VALOIS, ELPHÈGE (1894-   )
Yard artist, woodcarver   Causapascal, Matapèdia County, Québec
Working in a makeshift 'studio', he carved figures for sale, or for placement on his lawn. Subjects include various animals, birds, small human figures, usually standing, head, and groups of figures shown returning from a hunt or other anecdotal themes.

Ref: les patenteux du Québec

VAN ARSDALE, ISAAC (active 1869-1907)
Potter   Picton, Ontario
Succeeding Oren L. Ballard at Cornwall, he produced blue-decorated stoneware in partnership with David A. Flack, using a distinctively stylized bird motif. He had worked earlier at a pottery enterprise in New York State.

Ref: Kobayashi et al, *Folk Treasurers of Ontario*; Newlands, *Early Ontario Potters*;
     Webster, *Early Canadian Pottery*

VAN EE, PETER (1916-   )
Yard artist   Harriston, Ontario
The Van Ee family emigrated from Holland, settling at Arthur, Ontario, in the 1950s, then moving to Harriston. Following his retirement from farming he turned to woodcarving as a year-round hobby. His first project was a Dutch windmill, which he constructed beside the house. He later began to

make weathervanes, some with horse-and-carriage, others with roosters and other birds. He made miniature houses, birdhouses and garden ornaments. Nearly all of his work is colourful, painted in bright yellows and reds, as is his brick house on King Street.

212

Inf: Peter Van Ee

VAN IEPEREN, CORNELIUS (1899-   )
Painter   Consul, Saskatchewan

The Van Ieperens arrived in western Canada in 1912, settling in Saskatchewan. Cornelius started to paint in 1967, taking up the hobby as a pastime when he found himself severely confined by multiple sclerosis. He executed numerous oil paintings based frequently upon nostalgic recollections of days gone by or upon observation of contemporary details of life on the Prairies. Among works done in later life are paintings with the titles 'Steam Era', Steam Threshing Era', 'Early Morning Snack', 'Contentement', 'Exhaustion', 'Valley Farm', 'Saskatchewan Pioneer Visit' and 'Past Life Style in Saskatchewan Farming', all done in oil on canvasboard.

Ref: Grassroots Saskatchewan catalogue; From the Heart
Coll: Saskatchewan Arts Board

VAN LAMBALGEN, GERALD (1910-   )
Painter   Saskatoon, Saskatchewan

A self-taught artist, he nevertheless painted for virtually his entire life, having started when a child. Most of his works are done in oil on panel or oil on canvasboard. His subjects are rather diverse, including scenes of his Dutch homeland, childhood memories and contemporary observations in Saskatchewan. He did numerous copies or interpretations of the works of Old Masters, and once said, 'Vermeer is easy, but Rembrandt I can't do. I can do Hals'. Representative titles include 'Dutch Countryside', 'Little Town', 'Street Scene-Haarlem', 'Harvest', and 'Log House en Museum'.

Ref: Grassroots Saskatchewan catalogue
Coll: Saskatchewan Arts Board

VAUGHN, CLYDE (1922-   )
Woodcarver   Western Shore, Lunenburg County, Nova Scotia

Like many folk artists, Clyde Vaughn was a jack-of-all-trades who worked as a lumber millman, cooper and mason. When he took up storekeeping at Western Shore with his wife in 1973, he spent a year or so making rather special carvings of horses and cattle, painted and replete with wagons and other accoutrements. These were displayed for sale in the store. As is the case with many folk artists of the time, he found that sales did not encourage him to continue the long hours he had to invest in the work and he gradually became discouraged and gave up the work. To date, he is largely unknown outside of his community as a carver and only vaguely remembered there.

Inf: Chris Huntington

VERRET, OCTAVE (1902-1982)
Woodcarver   Edmunston, New Brunswick
He was born at Notre-Dame-du-Lac in Québec. The son of a flour miller who worked also at Trois-Pistoles, he learned to make shingles at age 16, and at age 23 lost a leg in an accident. In his later life he became a shoemaker and bought land near Edmunston, N.B. In town, he later ran a store. A stomach operation left him a near invalid, during which time he took up the pastime of making models patterned after farm vehicles and tools which he had used himself. Most of his models and other carvings were done between 1968 and 1974.

Ref: From the Heart; National Museum of Man Archives (CCFCS)
Coll: National Museum of Man (CCFCS)

VILLENEUVE, ARTHUR (1910-   )
Painter   Chicoutimi, Québec
Born into a family of labourers (his father was a brick-layer and carpenter), he worked at an early age in a paper mill, then as a 'chore-boy' in a lumber camp. Eventually he became a barber's apprentice at age 16, then bought his own barber shop at age 19. He was the victim of the economic collapse of the 1930s and was forced to sell his property, taking a job as hired barber at the Hôtel-Dieu hospital in Chicoutimi. His first modest artistic efforts date back to a few small drawings in a sketchbook, about 1946. At this time he tried model-building, making, among other things, a ship's model, a minia-ture house, a carved clock, and a never-finished sheet-metal model of the Québec Citadel. In 1956 he began to paint his house – doors, ceiling, walls, everything. In 1949 he opened his house to visitors, calling it his 'Le Musée

Villeneuve, Arthur (1910-   ). *Québec Village*. Oil on canvas: 1960s. Coll: National Museum of Man (CCFCS).

de l'artiste'. He had no schooling, and apparently no discernible influence from his artist-friends such as Alfred Pellan. He regarded his creative talent as God-given. He was at first ridiculed and his house was frequently vandalized, until his work was exhibited at the Waddington Gallery in 1961. His many oil paintings tend to reject realism, echoing his own comment, 'You can't copy or you're dead'. Some works are documentary in their subject matter, including town scenes and events from village life, while others are fantastic in nature. His technique entails the feature of large areas of strong colour enclosed within heavy, wavy outlines, giving the compositions a swirling, emotional appearance.

Ref: Gagnon, *Arthur Villeneuve's Québec Chronicles*; Harper, *A People's Art*
Coll: Art Gallery of Ontario; National Gallery of Canada; National Museum of Man (CCFCS)

VINCENT, ROBERT (1908-)
    Painter   Saskatoon, Saskatchewan
Robert Vincent is one of those artists who seems to fall somewhere in
between the categories of folk and trained artist. His training was minimal,
although his knowledge of technical processes was relatively sophisticated.
Born at Newcastle-on-Tyne in England, he emigrated to Canada in 1927. His
interest in painting stems from his youth, and he has said 'I was born with a
paintbrush in my mouth, instead of a silver spoon' (*Grassroots Saskatchewan*). He
was to execute a large number of works in lead pencil, oil and watercolour,
producing pictures of both country and town life, news events of the region
and western vistas of many types. These varied subjects are suggested by
titles such as 'Flooded Out – High River, Alberta', 'End of Roadwork', 'Saskatoon Broadway Bridge', 'Asphalt Plant, Sunday', or 'Co-op Refinery, Saskatoon'. His paintings reveal a particularly keen interest in the structures and
forms of buildings, vehicles and various objects.

Ref: Grassroots Saskatchewan Catalogue; *Robert Vincent: Selected Works 1950-1981*
Coll: The Gallery / Art Placement, Saskatoon; Mendel Art Gallery; Regina
    Public Library; Saskatchewan Arts Board

VINCENT, ZACHARIE (TELARION) (1812-1886)
    Painter   Lorette, Québec
Said to be the last pure-blood Huron, and chief of the Lorette Indian village
near Québec City, he is known for several oil paintings, including portraits
and self-portraits. The attempted formality of posture and background in his
works suggests that he had seen academic paintings whose conventions he
tried to imitate.

Ref: Harper, *Painters and Engravers*; Harper, *A People's Art*
Coll: Congregation of the Resurrection; Laval University, Musée du Québec

WAGNER, JOSEPH (active c. 1867-1880)
    Potter   Berlin (Kitchener), Ontario
He took over the operation of the pottery of his father Anselm in Berlin,
and produced a broad range of utilitarian earthenware jars and crocks. An
unusual feature which often serves to distinguish Wagner potter is the presence of hand-painted floral designs in green or blue slip, especially on jugs
and pitchers.

Ref: Newlands, *Early Ontario Potters*
Coll: Joseph Schneider Haus; National Museum of Man (History Division);
  Royal Ontario Museum (Sigmund Samuel Canadiana Collection

216 WALL, JAKE (1902-   )
  Model builder   Saskatoon, Saskatchewan
A retired farmer north of Saskatoon, Jake Wall had grown up in the Mennonite village of Neuhorst. After his retirement he took up a hobby, con-
ducted over a period of several years, of constructing a complete replica of
this Mennonite village, complete with the house-barns typical of the region,
fences, gardens and streets. The houses were constructed of cutout plywood
and brightly painted, while he used real straw in making roofs similar to
those actually constructed in pioneer times.

Ref: Bird and Kobayashi, A *Splendid Harvest*

WALLACE, AGNES PRINGLE (active 1840s)
  Embroiderer   St. Thomas, Ontario
While little is known of her life, she is the maker of an exceptionally fine
piece of embroidery work, done on a picture of Queen Victoria in 1841,
with painted work by her mother, Mary Ann Pringle (cf. Mary Ann McLean
Pringle).

Ref: Harper, A *People's Art* (catalogue)

WALPER, ORA C. (1881-1961)
  Painter   Kitchener, Ontario
A descendant of early continental German settlers who were successful
entrepreneurs in 19th-century Berlin (Kitchener), he was an amateur painter
of considerable skill. At mid-20th century he did an oil painting of the
founding of the city, based on accounts in local histories, notably that of Ezra
E. Eby, recording the Varnum Inn, the first business in the village.

Ref: Harper, *People's Art* (catalogue); Kobayashi, 'Local Paintings Tour Canada'
Coll: Kitchener Public Library

WALSH, EDWARD (1756-1832)
  Painter   Upper Canada (Ontario)
As a surgeon, Walsh's services were required on many tours of the British

Warin, George (1830-1904). Canada Goose Decoy. Painted wood: c. 1865.

army, including a period during which he was stationed in Canada for several years. He is known for his watercolour painting, A *View of York*, painted during his stay in 1803. He was also stationed at Montréal, Niagara and Detroit, sketching in each area. He did aquatint views of Montréal and Fort Erie in 1811, and other views of the Niagara frontier, some of which were used for book illustration.

Ref: Harper, *Painters and Engravers*; Harper, *People's Art* (catalogue)
Coll: Detroit Institute of Art; Royal Ontario Museum (Sigmund Samuel Canadiana Collection)

WARD, CHARLES CALEB (1831-1896)
    Painter   New Brunswick
He is known for paintings of the sea and of a historical subject, entitled 'Wreck in Quaco Bay, New Brunswick', signed and dated 1851.

Ref: Public Archives of Canada
Coll: Royal Ontario Museum (Sigmund Samuel Canadiana Collection)

WARIN, GEORGE (1830-1904)
    Decoy carver   Toronto, Ontario
Along with his brother James, he was a boat builder in Toronto, advertising the business as 'G. and J. Warin Boat Builders' on George Street in the 1870s. George Warin is the better known of the two because of his period of

Warning, Maria Beck (1832-1918). Hooked rug. Wool on burlap: 1893.

activity making decoys. After the formation of the boat-building partnership, the two brothers continued to make hollow-body decoys, usually stamped on the bottom. A prolific craftsman, George Warin is believed to have carved models of virtually every species of bird hunted in Ontario. Warin, Tom Chambers and Jack Wells are generally considered to be the originators of the 'Toronto School' of decoy makers.

Ref: Gates, *Ontario Decoys*; Kangas and Kangas, *Decoys: A North American Survey*

WARNER, WILLIAM (active 1856-c. 1860)
    Potter   Toronto, Ontario
Warner was among numerous American-born craftsmen who had previously worked in New Jersey and New York prior to coming to Canada. The Warner Pottery produced blue-decorated stoneware with floral and even some animal designs. The pottery was of short duration, and financial failure forced its closing within a few years of its beginning.

Ref: Newlands, *Early Ontario Potters*

WARNING, MARIA BECK (1832-1918)
    Rug maker   Brunner, Perth County, Ontario
When the vogue for rug hooking made itself felt in Canada in the late 19th century, Maria Warning was already a comparatively elderly woman. For

approximately ten years, between c. 1884 and 1892 or so, she made a number of extraordinarily fine rugs, all featuring birds or animals, and most with geometric borders and year of making. One of her outstanding designs was a tall, crowing rooster, used at least twice, one with a border of alternating diagonal colours, the other framed within a composition of tulips and hearts.

Ref: Bird and Kobayashi, A *Splendid Harvest*

WARRE, HENRY JAMES (1819-1898)
Topographical artist   Eastern Canada
As an officer in the British army Warre travelled across Canada, recording many views along the way. Occasional examples of work feature a simplicity which serves to distinguish them from the empirical precision of most topographical art. His sketches were to appear as coloured lithographs, entitled *Sketches in North America and the Oregon Territory*, published in London in 1848.

Ref: Harper, *Painters and Engravers*; *Heritage of Brant*
Coll: Art Gallery of Ontario; National Gallery of Canada;
   Public Archives of Canada

WARTERS, WINIFRED (1898-1963)
Painter   Winnipeg, Manitoba
A self-taught artist, she did a number of oil paintings of scenes in Winnipeg, painted in her later years. One of the best-known examples of her work is a picture of the old Winnipeg downtown, based largely upon memory and anecdote, in that it includes long-extinct shops and depicts the streets filled with Christmas revellers and Indians gathered around a teepee.

Ref: Harper, A *People's Art*

WATERHOUSE, ROBERT (active 1930s)
Decoy carver   Verdun, Québec
One of a group of skillful decoy-makers at Verdun, Robert Waterhouse is known for a considerable diversity of forms. Several ducks and a blue-wing teal which he made in the 1930s exhibit refined painting in combination with extensively-carved details.

Ref: Kangas and Kangas; *Decoys: A North American Survey*

Watson, Josephus (1792-after 1857). Testimonial. Watercolour and ink on paper: 1857.

WATSON, JOSEPHUS (1792-after 1857)

Calligrapher, painter   Toronto, Ontario
Among the participants in William Lyon Mackenzie's abortive revolt against
the 'Family Compact' in 1837, Josephus Watson was arrested and thrown
into Toronto Jail. Like others expecting to be executed for the crime of
treason, Watson inscribed on a small pine box a memento to his wife and
children, fearing that he would not see them again. He was eventually par-
doned, much to his own surprise. Some twenty years later he meticulously
lettered an elaborate testimonial in which he recalled the major events of
his life, and composed a meditation upon the ingredients of personal and
social well-being. He also traced his ancestral lineage, and recorded his own
titles and achievements, describing himself as 'mechanic, student of Arts and
Sciences, Engineer and Patenter of a Bedstead for the Sick, also Engineer and
Patenter of divers improvements on Ploughs'. Accompanying this sustained
text is an array of meticulously drawn arms, symbols, geometric designs and
decorative details rendered in both ink and watercolour.

Inf: Vernon and Maggie Smart
Ref: Kobayashi et al, *Folk Treasures of Historic Ontario*

WEBER, ANNA (1814-1888)

Fraktur artist   Waterloo County, Ontario
Anna Weber was born in Earl Township, Lancaster County, in 1814 at a time
when many Mennonites were pulling up their Pennsylvania roots to migrate
northward. The Weber family joined this exodus in 1825, settling just north
of the village of Waterloo. Never married, and apparently suffering from a
number of physical ailments, she was taken into the homes of many families
throughout her life. Her fraktur career was most likely born out of the
motive of consolation and of the desire to extend tokens of appreciation to
her hosts and visitors. Over a 22-year period she produced many charming
watercolour drawings of traditional Pennsylvania-German folk art subjects,
including flowers, birds, hearts, geometric designs and domestic animals. Her
earliest dated work is her own Mennonite hymn-book, whose inside cover
bears a simple drawing of a bird, her signature and the date 1866. Most of
her drawings are done in symmetrical arrangements of motifs, and nearly all
are signed and dated to the precise day. Some also contain the names of recipients, many of them young children to whom Anna Weber presented
these pictures. A prolific artist, she probably painted upwards of a hundred
pictures, including several examples done in the final months before her
death in 1888.

Weber, Anna (1814-1888). Fraktur drawing. Watercolour on paper: 1870.

Ref: Bird, *Ontario Fraktur*; Bird and Kobayashi, A *Splendid Harvest*; Good, E. Reginald, *Anna's Art*; Harper, A *People's Art*; Patterson, Nancy-Lou, 'Anna Weber'

Coll: Conrad Grebel College Archives; Joseph Schneider Haus Museum; National Museum of Man (CCFCS); St. Catharines Historical Museum; York County (Pennsylvania) Historical Society

WEBER, JACOB (active 1873-1897)
Potter   Egmondville, Huron County, Ontario
A German immigrant to Ontario after mid-century, he entered into partnership with his father-in-law, Valentine Boehler, in the operation of the Huron Pottery after 1873. He continued to decorate earthenwares with applied flowers and blue painted floral motifs until the end of the 19th century.

Ref: Newlands, *Early Ontario Potters*
Coll: Royal Ontario Museum (Sigmund Samuel Canadiana Collection)

WEBSTER, CLARENCE (c. 1900-   )
Painter   Toronto, Ontario
Born in Hawaii, Clarence was adopted at age four by Halifax parents. He expressed an early desire to travel, and by age 15 joined the Merchant Marine, virtually sailing around the world. Throughout his life he was inclined toward solitary living, and he never married. His adventures took him to many parts of Canada and the world, including at least one brief period spent in prison. Although he may always have done some drawing, his greatest artistic output appears to have occurred when he was confined to nursing homes in Toronto. He used his art at one time as a means to brighten up a dreary room, drawing with pencil and crayons on the dry wall partions. After his move from this institution, it was demolished, and the wall was saved, cut up into panels containing several of his pictures. Resettled in a new home, the nursing staff provided him with paper and felt markers, enabling him to pursue his pastime in earnest. His drawings are usually depictions of people eating, playing cards or visiting in rooms, enclosed within floral borders. His work became known to the public when it was exhibited at a Toronto gallery in a show of primitive art.

Inf: Ralph and Patricia Price
Ref: Kobayashi et al, *Folk Treasures of Historic Ontario*; McKendry, *Folk Art*
Coll: National Museum of Man (CCFCS)

Webster, Clarence (c. 1900-   ). *Centennial Garden Party*. Felt marker on paper: c. 1975.

WEILER, MARTIN (1908-   )

Yard artist   Waterloo, Ontario

Known also as 'Mike', Martin Weiler had originally lived and worked in Maryhill before retiring to Waterloo. He undertook a project of several years in making whirligigs, weathervanes, windmills and whimseys of all sorts in his yard and shed. Most of his pieces are conceived around a humorous idea, as, for example, a 'chain saw' comprised of a saw handle and a chain, or an 'electric cork puller' made with an ordinary augur attached to a length of electrical cord. Other whirligigs are made in the forms of boats and trains.

Inf: Martin Weiler

WEIR, GEORGE (RED) (1890s-1978)
Decoy carver   Hamilton, Ontario
Son of a Hamilton boatbuilder, 'Red' Weir owned a boat house on the
north shore of Hamilton Bay which served as his workshop. He carved many
decoys for hunters of the western Lake Ontario region. Most of these were   225
hollow decoys with a rough textured finish to reduce glare on sunny days of
when wet. Many of his decoys are distinguished by exceptionally fine
painted finishes.

Ref: Gates, Ontario Decoys

WELDING, WILLIAM E. (active 1867-1894)
Potter   Brantford, Ontario
Beginning as a salesman for the Brantford Pottery firm, he was eventually to
become one of the most active craftsmen and entrepreneurs of this long-
lasting establishment. He produced a wide variety of stoneware, ranging
from the sophistication of elaborate picture frames to the simplicity of
storage crocks. Many of the latter, as well as special miniature pieces, were
decorated with blue flowers and other designs.

Ref: Kobayashi et al, Folk Treasures of Ontario; Newlands, Early Ontario Potters
Coll: Brantford Museum; Royal Ontario Museum (Sigmund Samuel Canadiana
    Collection)

WELLS, MRS. FARLEY (c. 1900-   )
Woodcarver   Franktown, Ontario
Turning to woodcarving as a pastime in her later years, she began whittling
of birds, animals, fish and other subjects. She began to work at more complex projects, including a carved replica of the famous Carlsberg horse team
and beer wagon. Using pine or other softwoods, she had made numerous
models and carved a wide range of subjects for her own amusement and
showing at local fairs.

Ref: National Museum of Man Archives (CCFCS)

WELLS, J.R. (JACK) (1880s-1953)
Decoy carver   Toronto, Ontario
Like George Warin, Wells was a boat-builder on the Toronto waterfront,
and found occasion to carve decoys for hunters in the region. Most active

during the period 1910-1935, he was an active craftsman, producing many
hollow and solid decoys, sometimes featuring his initials stamped on the
base. His work is recognizable for its refinement of carved and painted
detail, not unlike that of Warin, by whom he was likely influenced.

Ref: Gates, Ontario Decoys

WERNER, ALICE (1913-   )
    Painter   Mikado district, Saskatchewan
As with many other self-taught artists, her entry into painting did not occur
until comparatively late in life. She first began to do drawings and paintings
in 1967, and continued at an active pace for several years afterward. Her subjects tend to be local or anecdotal in nature.

Ref: Saskatchewan Arts Board
Coll: Saskatchewan Arts Board

WETTLAUFER, ECKHARDT (1845-1919)
    Wagonmaker, painter   Sebastopol, Ontario
Eckhardt Wettlaufer had operated a wagon-making shop, cider mill and
other enterprises in the Sebastopol vicinity of Oxford and Perth counties
into the early 20th century. He was a highly capable practitioner of the art
of stencilling. In the late 19th century he decorated children's wagons,
including five special wagons for his grandchildren. A particularly decorative
piece, made c. 1875 for his four-year old son Adam, is a crokinole board with
stylized tulip-motifs painted against a rich four-colour background.

Inf: Oscar and Clara Wettlaufer
Ref: Bird and Kobayashi, A Splendid Harvest
Coll: Joseph Schneider Haus Museum

WHALE, ROBERT (1805-1887)
    Painter   Burford, Ontario
Born on a farm at Alternum, Cornwell, he studied for a time in London but
was mainly self-taught. In his childhood he attempted several portraits,
inspired by the formal works of Reynolds, seen in the museums of London.
He emigrated to Canada in 1852, settling at Burford. He painted numerous
portraits and landscapes in the Brantford district and along the Grand River.
He also painted in the Maritime Provinces and in New England. He became a

member of ARCA in 1881. For all of his attainments of wide recognition, he was essentially a self-taught artist who developed exceptional competence. Occasional works betray simplifications of technique in marked contrast to the formal rigour of many of his pictures.

Ref: Harper, *A People's Art; Heritage of Brant*
Coll: Art Gallery of Brant; London Regional Art Gallery; National Gallery of
    Canada; Royal Ontario Museum (Sigmund Samuel Canadiana Collection)

WHEELER, BILLY
    Furniture maker, woodcarver   Keels, Bonavista Bay, Newfoundland
A fisherman by trade, Billy Wheeler became a furniture maker simply out of the desire to make for himself what he would otherwise have to buy. He constructed several chairs, settees, couches, commodes and other pieces for himself and his neighbours in and around Keels. Numerous inventive carved panels and architectural details throughout his small house exhibit details of workmanship similar to those on his distinctive furniture.

Ref: Peddle, *The Traditional Furniture of Outport Newfoundland*

WILE, HARRY (1891-1978)
    Woodcarver   Lunenburg County, Nova Scotia
Harry was a woodsman all of his life and worked as a cook for camps in Ontario. Like many who followed the lumberjack life, he carried a knife to make ax handles and the occasional carving. Upon retirement in 1966, he began to make numerous carvings, mostly of horse and ox teams, sulkies, etc. His work was not particularly refined, but had great character. He had only one eye and in old age he found working difficult, but kept going until the end. A fair number of his pieces are still in Lunenburg County houses.

Inf: Chris Huntington
Coll: Art Gallery of Nova Scotia

WILLIAMS, ARCH (1909-   )
    Painter   Ferryland, Newfoundland
The best-known of Newfoundland folk painters, he was born at Ferryland. He worked for seventeen years as a fisherman, then thirty-one years as community bookkeeper. In later years he became involved in civic matters as clerk of the Community Council, and a founder of the Ferryland Historical

Winterborn, James (active 1860s). *Roxburgh Place*. Watercolour on paper: 1868.

Society. A self-taught artist, he began painting seriously in 1970, prodded by the painter and sculptor Gerry Squires who had moved from western Canada and bought a painting. His pictures are based variously upon memory and observation of scenery and events in the Ferryland area. He painted many landscapes and ocean scenes of communities of the Southern Shore, sometimes with the aid of old photographs.

Ref: Folk Images '77 Five Newfoundland Folk Painters

WILLIAMSON, Stan (1877-1968)
Woodcarver, model builder   Gananoque, Ontario
Stan Williamson was a man of many skills. He was best known in his life as a stonecutter who made tombstones in Gananoque. In later life he busied himself with the making of various boat models and carved figures, as well as paintings which he exhibited at Fall fairs. One of his most elaborate under-takings is his model of a village street showing townspeople engage in vari-ous professional activities. He made numerous models of ships and smaller

boats, some with carved human figures, inspired by watching various craft come into harbour on the St. Lawrence Seaway.

Inf: Stephen Inglis
Ref: From the Heart
Coll: National Museum of Man (CCFCS)

WILSON, ROBERT 'SCOTTIE' (1890-1972)
 Painter   Toronto, Ontario
'Scottie' Wilson was, in a sense, a traveller through Canada who left an artistic legacy during his stay here. Born in Glasgow, he went to work at an early age before volunteering for the army. He later emigrated to Canada and opened a shop in Toronto. He began to immerse himself in drawing around 1942. His drawings, many done in watercolour and crayon, have an Escher-like quality in that they entail interplay of figure and ground, fit pieces fitting together like a puzzle. He eventually returned to England where he was heralded as a modern primitive artist.

Ref: Harper, A People's Art

WINTER, HENRY WILLIAM
 Furniture maker   Clarke's Beach, Conception Bay, Newfoundland
A self-taught commercial furniture-maker, he and his single assistant produced a considerable quantity of furniture, much of which was based upon late Victorian and Eastlake styles, from c. 1890-1935. One of the most unusual pieces made by Winter is a large sideboard for the Roman Catholic Rectory at Brigus, with its profusion of applied half-spindles and decorative shell-carving on drawers and arcades.

Ref: Peddle, The Traditional Furniture of Outport Newfoundland

WINTERBORN, JAMES (active 1860s)
 Painter   Oxford County, Ontario
A schoolteacher and amateur artist, James Winterborn was most likely an itinerant painter who offered his services to land owners who might wish to have an artistic record of their estates. On the basis of known works he appears to have worked in Oxford and Waterloo counties, where he did several large watercolour landscapes of farmsteads, depicting substantial homes, livestock, and other evidence of prosperous farming activity. In the

Wren, Bernie (1917-   ). *There's a Whisper of Wind*. Painted wood: c. 1977.
Coll: National Museum of Man (CCFCS).

manner of amateur artists, details are carefully developed, almost without regard to overall composition. He uses strong linear arrangements and vibrant colours in his dramatic works.

Ref: Bird, *Canadian Folk Art*; Dobson and Dobson, A *Provincial Elegance*

WOODALL, MRS. I. (active 1930s)
    Sculptor   Toronto, Ontario
She worked with Mrs. A. Hewitson to make a miniature orchestra of crepe paper and cardboard, exhibited at the Women's Building, Canadian National Exhibition, where it won first prize for the years 1933-37.
(See HEWITSON, MRS. A.)

Ref: Waddington's catalogue (November 9-11, 1981)

WREN, BERNIE (1917-   )
    Woodcarver, painter   Langley, British Columbia
After retiring from hard work in logging camps in western Canada, he used his leisure time to draw upon his years of experience in the forests, making relief carvings of events associated with the forest industry. He carved and painted a series of scenes depicting details of climbing, cutting and logging, as well as views of the British Columbia mountain country with trees, lakes and log houses. He had begun his artistic pursuit by painting in 1975, but soon shifted his energies to carving, a form he found more satisfying, and retained for him some contact with the wood which he had approached in a working capacity earlier. His high relief carving and strong colours of blue, green and orange give considerable visual impact to his pictures.

Ref: From the Heart
Coll: National Museum of Man (CCFCS)

WYERS, JAN G. (1888-1973)
    Painter   Windhorst, Saskatchewan
He was born at Steeneren, the Netherlands, and died in 1973 at Regina, Saskatchewan. He emigrated to Canada in 1916, settling at Windhorst. He undertook painting in a serious way during the Great Depression, depicting scenes of by-gone days with nostalgic enthusiasm. He painted many recollec- tions of life in Holland, as well as rural scenes of western Canada. His pictures frequently depict moments in the working day on a Prairie farm, showing

Wyers, Jan (1888-1973). *These Good Old Threshing Days*. Oil on fabric: c. 1957.
Coll: Norman Mackenzie Art Gallery.

horses drinking at quitting time, or the flurry of activity associated with threshing, harnessing the collective energies of men and their machines. Among titles of his various works are 'Those Good Old Threshing Days', 'Horse Parade', 'My Home in Holland', and 'The Homecoming'. Working in oil, he painted in rich, warm colours.

Ref: Harper, *A People's Art*; *Prairie Folk Art*
Coll: Norman McKenzie Art Gallery; Saskatchewan Arts Board

WYLIE, ROBERT (active 1970s and after)
   Sculptor   Thomasburg, Ontario
The Celtic background of this capable craftsman became especially apparent with artistic projects which he began to undertake when in his 50s. Among these endeavours are several crosses which he carved from hardwood, utilizing decorative motifs derived from early stone gravemarkers found throughout the British Isles. On occasion Wylie depicted also the crucified

Christ, wearing the cloak of Resurrection, with traditional decorative embellishment of clothing and background. Most of the crosses are small enough to place on or over a table, while at least one known superbly carved example stands nearly two metres in height.

Inf: Ralph and Patricia Price
Ref: Kobayashi et al, Folk Treasures of Historic Ontario; McKendry, Folk Art

YORKE, SIR JOSEPH SYDNEY (1768-1831)
   Topographer   Eastern Canada
An amateur topographical artist, Yorke served as a volunteer in the Royal Navy for several years. He spent a brief time at Newfoundland Station and Halifax in the 1780s, and is known by a least one monochrome watercolour painting which he executed in Newfoundland in 1786.

Ref: Harper, Painters and Engravers

ZIEGLER, ALFRED (active 1960s and after)
   Woodcarver   Hanover, Ontario
An amateur whittler and carver, Alfred Ziegler took up the pursuit to fill idle hours in later life. He constructed various models of horses, human figures, wagons and implements. He is particularly known by a carved and painted chuck wagon and four-horse team, inscribed 'Calgary Stampede 1965'. He also carved and assembled buggies and other horse-drawn vehicles.

Ref: National Museum of Man (CCFCS), Thomas Lackey file)

Bibliography

Adamson, Anthony, and Willard, John. *The Gaiety of Gables: Ontario's Architectural Folk Art.* Toronto: McClelland and Stewart, 1974.

The Art of Frank Kocevar. Burnaby, British Columbia: The Simon Fraser Gallery, 1975.

Arthur Villeneuve's Québec Chronicles. Montréal: The Montréal Museum of Fine Art, 1972.

Arts populaires du Québec. Québec: Musée du Québec, 1975.

Avann, Keith. 'Cliff Avann, Decoy Maker.' *The Upper Canadian* (May / June, 1985), pp. 12-14.

Barbeau, Marius. 'Are the Real Folk Arts and Crafts Dying Out?' *Canadian Art* (Winter, 1948), pp. 128-133.

————. *I Have Seen Québec.* Toronto: Macmillan of Canada, 1957.

————. *Louis Jobin Statuaire.* Montréal: Librairie Beauchemin Limitée, 1968.

————. *Québec – Where Ancient France Lingers.* Toronto: Macmillan of Canada, 1936.

————. 'Two Centuries of French-Canadian Wood Carving.' *Canadian Forum* (March, 1936), pp. 24-25.

Barrett, Harry B. *Lore and Legends of Long Point.* Don Mills, Ontario: Burns and MacEachern, 1977.

Barss, Peter. *Older Ways: Traditional Nova Scotia Craftsmen.* Toronto: Van Nostrand Reinhold, 1980.

Bird, Michael S. *Canadian Folk Art: Old Ways in a New Land.* Toronto: Oxford University Press, 1983.

————. 'Christian L. Hoover (1835-1918): Markham Township Fraktur Artist.' *Canadian Collector* (July / August, 1977), pp. 28-31.

————. *Folk Art: A Sampling of Decorative Works from the Region, the Province, the Country.* Cambridge, Ontario: The Gallery & Library, 1984.

————. *Ontario Fraktur: A Pennsylvania German Folk Tradition in Early Canada.* Toronto: M.F. Feheley, 1977.

————. 'Ontario Fraktur.' *The Magazine Antiques* (September, 1983), pp. 538-546.

————. 'Perpetuation and Adaptation: The Furniture and Craftsmanship of John Gemeinhardt (1826-1912).' *Canadian Antiques and Art Review* (March, 1981), pp. 19-34.

————. 'Survival Transcended: Folk Art in Canada.' *Canadian Collector* (September, 1983), pp. 48-51.

Bird, Michael, and Kobayashi, Terry. *A Splendid Harvest: Germanic Folk and Decorative Arts in Canada.* Toronto: Van Nostrand Reinhold, 1981.

Bonner, Mary Graham. *Made in Canada.* New York: Knopf, 1943.

Bouchard, Laurent. *Courtepointes Québécois.* Québec: Ministere des Affaires culturelles, 1977.

Brochu, Brenda, 'Robert Vincent: A Matter of Insight.' Saskatoon: *Commentator* (January 28, 1970), p. 16.

Burgess, Evelyn W. 'The Dolls of John Halfyard.' *Westworld* (September / October, 1976), pp. 18-20.

Burnham, Harold B., and Burnham, Dorothy K. *Keep Me Warm One Night:*

Early Handweaving in Canada. Toronto: University of Toronto Press, 1972.

Carpenter, Carole Henderson. *Many Voices: A Study of Folklore Activities in Canada and Their Role in Canadian Culture*. Ottawa: National Museums of Canada, 1979.

Celebration: The Marjorie Larmon Collection: 19th & 20th Century Folk Art in Canada. Windsor: Art Gallery of Windsor, 1982.

Charlie Tanner Retrospective. Art Gallery of Nova Scotia, 1984.

Conroy, Mary. *Canada's Quilts*. Toronto: Griffen House Press, 1976.

Contemporary Primitives. Kingston: The Agnes Etherington Art Centre, 1982.

Cumming, Mark. *The Group of One: Joseph Bradshaw Thorne*. Stratford, Ontario: Cumming Publishers, 1981.

Day, Peter, 'Roadside Attractions.' *Canadian Art* (Spring, 1985), pp. 42-51.

Decorated Nova Scotia Furnishings. Halifax: Dalhousie Art Gallery, 1978.

Dmytro Stryjek. Saskatoon: Mendel Art Gallery, 1982 (Essays by Lynne S. Bell, George Moppett).

Dobson, Henry, and Dobson, Barbara. *The Early Furniture of Ontario and the Atlantic Provinces*. Toronto: M.F. Feheley, 1974.

———. *A Provincial Elegance: Arts of the Early French and English Settlements in Canada*. Kitchener: Kitchener-Waterloo Art Gallery, 1982.

Dupont, Jean-Claude. *Historie populaire de l'Acadie*. Ottawa: Les Éditions Leméac, Inc., 1978.

Dwyer, Ruth. *Mennonite Decorative Arts*. Hamilton: McMaster University Art Gallery, 1981.

Eastern Canadian Quilts and Hooked Rugs of the 19th and Early 20th Centuries. Uxbridge, Ontario: Uxbridge-Scott Historical Society, 1978.

Exhibition of Canadian Gamesboards of the Nineteenth and Twentieth Centuries from Ontario, Québec and Nova Scotia, An. Halifax: Art Gallery of Nova Scotia, 1981 (Essays by Richard Field, Elliott Avedon).

Fabric of Their Lives: Hooked and Poked Mats of Newfoundland and Labrador, The. St. John's: Memorial University of Newfoundland Art Gallery, 1980.

Ferryland Folk Art: Arch Williams. St. John's: Memorial University of Newfoundland Art Gallery, 1975.

Fleming, Patricia, 'In Search of the Work of William G. Loney, 1878-1956.' *The Upper Canadian* (November / December, 1983), pp. 29-30.

Flights of Fancy: Newfoundland Yard Art. St. John's: Memorial University Art Gallery, 1983 (Essays by Gerald L. Pocius, Patricia Grattan).

'Folk Art: Sidney Howard, Woodcarver.' *Canada Crafts* 3 (August / September, 1978), pp. 19-21.

Folk Art in Canada. Plattsburg, New York: Clinton County Historical Association, 1981. (Essay by Joan I. Mattie).

Folk Art of Nova Scotia. Halifax: Art Gallery

of Nova Scotia, 1977 (Essays by Bernard Riordan, Marie Elwood).

Folk Art Treasures of Québec. Québec: Ministère des affaires culturelles, 1980.

Folk Painters of the Canadian West. Ottawa: National Gallery of Canada, 1960.

Folk Images '77. St. John's: Memorial University of Newfoundland Art Gallery, 1977 (Essay by Patricia Grattan).

Foss, Charles H., and Vroom, Richard. *Cabinetmakers of the Eastern Seaboard: A Study of Early Canadian Furniture*. Toronto: M.F. Feheley, 1977.

Francis Silver, 1841-1920. Halifax: Art Gallery of Nova Scotia, 1982 (Essay by Bernard Riordan).

From the Heart: Folk Art in Canada. Toronto: McClelland and Stewart, 1983. (In conjunction with travelling exhibition from National Museum of Man, Canadian Centre for Folk Culture Studies).

Gates, Bernard. *Ontario Decoys*. Kingston, Ontario: Private Printing, 1982.

Gioia, Louis J. 'Edouard Jasmin at Prime Canadian Crafts.' *artmagazine* (December, 1980), pp. 53-54.

Glenbow Collects. Calgary, Alberta: Glenbow Museum.

Good, E. Reginald. *Anna's Art*. Kitchener, Ontario: Private Printing, 1976.

Good Heavens: Conrad Furey, Lynda Lapeer, Gordon Law, George Steadman. Oshawa: The Robert MacLaughlin Gallery, 1981.

'Grassroots Art.' *Artscanada* (December, 1969), entire issue.

Grassroots Saskatchewan. Regina, Saskatchewan: Norman Mackenzie Art Gallery, 1976.

Grattan, Patricia. '"A Pastime That's All": Primitive Painting in Newfoundland.' *Arts Atlantic* (Fall, 1977), pp. 14-17.

Griffiths, Ruth. 'Quality Work in Zone Art Competition.' *Prince Albert Herald* (February 24, 1982) (on William Laczko).

Grosbois, Louise de; Lamothe, Raymonde; and Nantel, Lise. *Les patenteux du Québec*. Montréal: Parti-Pris, 1974.

Guyette, Gary, and Guyette, Dale. *Decoys of Maritime Canada*. Exton, Pennsylvania: Schiffer Publishing Ltd., 1983.

Hanks, Carole. *Early Ontario Gravestones*. Toronto: McGraw-Hill Ryerson Ltd., 1974.

Harper, J. Russell. 'Folk Sculpture of Rural Québec: the Nettie Sharpe Collection.' *The Magazine Antiques* (April, 1973), pp. 724-733.

————. *Painters and Engravers in Early Canada*.

Harper, J. Russell. *Painting in Canada: A History*. Toronto: University of Toronto Press, 1966.

————. *A People's Art: Primitive, Naive, Provincial and Folk Painting in Canada*. Toronto: University of Toronto Press, 1974.

————. *People's Art*. Ottawa: National Gallery of Canada, 1973.

Heritage of Brant. Brantford, Ontario: Art Gallery of Brant, 1977.

Hill, Charles C. *Canadian Painting in the Thirties*. Ottawa: The National Gallery of Canada, 1975.

238 *Images de Charlevoix 1784-1950*. Montréal: Musée des beaux-arts de Montréal, 1982.

Images of Sport in Early Canada. Montréal: McCord Museum, 1976.

Imaginary Portrait, The: The Work of Hertha Muyson. Kingston: Agnes Etherington Centre, 1974.

Inglis, Stephen. *Something Out of Nothing: The Work of George Cockayne*. Ottawa: National Museum of Man Mercury Series, 1983.

Ivan Law Carvings. Oshawa: The Robert McLaughlin Gallery, 1978.

James, John W. 'Alfred Riggs: Sculptor or Whittler?' *The Atlantic Advocate* (July, 1975), pp. 13-15.

———. 'The Last Woodcarver of Old Saint John.' *The Atlantic Advocate* (June, 1974), pp. 65-71 (on John Rogerson).

Joe Norris: Paintings and Furniture. Halifax: Dalhousie Art Gallery, 1978 (Essay by Chris Huntington).

Joe Sleep Retrospective. Halifax: Art Gallery of Nova Scotia, 1981 (Essays by Bruce Ferguson, Harold Pearse).

Johannesen, Stanley, and Bird, Michael. *Furniture and Fraktur: An Exhibition of Artifacts from Waterloo County and Germanic Ontario*. Waterloo, Ontario: University of Waterloo Art Gallery, 1977.

Kangas, Gene, and Kangas, Linda. *Decoys: A North American Survey*. Spanish Fork, Utah: Hillcrest Publications, n.d.

Kobayashi, Terry. 'David B. Horst (1873-1965): St. Jacobs Woodcarver.' *Waterloo Historical Society* (1977), pp. 78-92.

———. 'Folk Art in Stone: Pennsylvania German Gravemarkers in Ontario.' *Waterloo Historical Society* (1982), pp. 90-113.

———. 'Fred G. Hoffman (1845-1926): Waterloo County Itinerant Woodcarver.' *Waterloo Historical Society* (1981), pp. 111-126.

———. 'Local Paintings Tour Canada: Ora C. Walper and J.J. Kenyon.' *Waterloo Historical Society* (1974), pp. 26-29.

Kobayashi, Terry; Bird, Michael; Price, Elizabeth. *Folk Treasures of Ontario*. Toronto: Ontario Heritage Foundation, 1985.

Law, Gordon. *Myth Poems*. Oshawa, Ontario: Private Printing, n.d.

Lessard, Michel, and Marquis, Huguette. *L'art traditionnel au Québec*. Montréal: Éditions de l'Homme, 1975.

Lessard, Michel. *Complete Guide to French-Canadian Antiques*. Translated by Elizabeth Abbott. New York: Hart, 1974.

Lesser, Gloria, and Foulem, Léopold L. 'Edouard Jasmin: Folk Ceramicist.' *The Studio Potter* (December, 1984), pp. 72-76.

Ludwig Flancer. Toronto: Home Again Gallery, 1981.

Macdonald, Colin S. A *Dictionary of Canadian Artists.*

Maclaren, George. *Antique Furniture by Nova Scotia Craftsmen.* Toronto: McGraw-Hill Ryerson, 1975.

Macnair, Peter; Hoover, Alan L.; and Neary, Kevin. *The Legacy: Continuing Traditions of Canadian Northwest Coast Indian Art.* Victoria: British Columbia Provincial Museum, 1980.

Mattie, Wesley C. 'Museum of Man Folk Art Collection.' *Canadian Antiques and Art Review* (November, 1979), pp. 26-31.

Mattie, Wesley C., and Klymasz, Robert B. 'Discovering the Art and Architecture of Birdhouses in Canada.' *Canadian Collector* (May / June, 1977), pp. 22-25.

McKendry, Blake. 'Arthur Sauve – Folk Artist.' *The Upper Canadian* (November / December, 1983), pp. 15-16.

————. *Folk Art: Primitive and Naive Art in Canada.* Toronto: Methuen, 1983.

McKendry, Ruth. *Quilts and Other Bed Coverings in the Canadian Tradition.* Toronto: Van Nostrand Reinhold, 1979.

McMurray, A. Lynn. 'Ontario German Decorative Arts.' In Donald B. Webster, *The Book of Canadian Antiques.* Toronto: McGraw-Hill Ryerson, 1974, pp. 128-142.

Millard, Peter. 'Dmytro Stryjek: Innovative Folk Painting.' *Artswest 6* (September, 1981), pp. 26-29.

Morgan, Patrick. 'Folk Painters of Charlevoix.' *Canadian Art* (Summer, 1947), pp. 152-155.

Newlands, David L. *Early Ontario Potters: Their Craft and their Trade.* Toronto: McGraw-Hill Ryerson, 1979.

Pain, Howard. *The Heritage of Upper Canadian Furniture: A Study in the Survival of Formal and Vernacular Styles from Britain, America and Europe, 1780-1900.* Toronto: Van Nostrand Reinhold, 1978.

Painting in Alberta. Edmonton: Edmonton Art Gallery.

Palardy, Jean. *The Early Furniture of French Canada.* Toronto: Macmillan of Canada, 1963.

Patterson, Nancy-Lou Gellerman. 'Anna Weber Hat das Gemacht: Anna Weber (1814-1888): A Fraktur Painter of Waterloo County, Ontario.' *Mennonite Life* (December, 1975), pp. 15-19.

————. *Mennonite Folk Art of Waterloo County.* Waterloo, Ontario: University of Waterloo Art Gallery, 1966.

————. *Mennonite Traditional Arts of the Waterloo Region and Southern Ontario: A Historical View.* Kitchener: Kitchener-Waterloo Art Gallery, 1974.

————. *Swiss-German and Dutch-German Mennonite Traditional Art in the Waterloo Region, Ontario.* Ottawa: National Museum of Man Mercury Series, 1979.

Patterson, Nancy-Lou Gellerman, and Bird, Michael. *A Germanic Flavour: Folk Art of the Waterloo Region and Other Germanic Settlements of Canada.* Kitchener-Waterloo Art Gallery, 1979.

240

———. *Primitive and Folk Art.* Waterloo, Ontario: University of Waterloo Art Gallery, 1976.

Pearse, Harold. 'Joe Norris.' *Vanguard* (November, 1984), pp. 32-33.

Peddle, Walter W. 'Conception Bay Furniture Maker.' *Canadian Collector* (November / December, 1982), pp. 19-23.

———. 'Newfoundland Outport Furniture: An Interpretation.' *Material History Bulletin* (Fall, 1980), pp. 19-35.

———. 'Newfoundland Outport Furniture.' *Canadian Antiques and Art Review* (September, 1980), pp. 39-41.

———. 'Outport Tailor-Made Furniture.' *Canadian Collector* (January / February, 1982), pp. 23-26.

———. *The Traditional Furniture of Outport Newfoundland.* St. John's: Harry Cuff Publications, 1983.

Percival, Robert. 'The Folk Paintings of Agnes McLaughlin.' *ArtsAtlantic* (Summer, 1981), pp. 31-32.

Playful Objects: An Exhibition in Celebration of Fun. Edmonton: Alberta Culture, 1980 (Essay by Jane Thomas).

Pocius, Gerald L. 'Calvert: A Study of Artifacts and Spatial Usage in a Newfoundland Community.' Ph.D. Dissertation: University of Pennsylvania, 1979.

———. 'Newfoundland Traditional Crafts: Types and Sterotypes.' *Artisan* 4, no. 5 (1981), pp. 15-20.

Porter, John R., and Désy, Léopold. *Calvaires et croix de chemins du Québec.* Montréal: Hurtibise, 1973.

'Prairie Folk Art.' *Artscanada* (October

November, 1979), entire issue.

Prairie Suite. Saskatoon: Shoestring Gallery, 1979.

Richardson, E.P. 'The Arts of French Canada.' *Canadian Art* (November, 1946), pp. 16-18.

Robert Vincent: Selected Works, 1950-1981. Saskatoon: Mendel Art Gallery, 1984 (Essay by Peter Millard).

Robert, Guy. *Lemieux.* Toronto: Gage Publishing, 1978.

Rowan, Michael. 'John L. Chappell, Folk Carver.' *East Georgian Bay Historical Journal* (Volume I), pp. 152-155.

Rupp, David W. 'The B. Lent Pottery c. 1836-1841.' *Canadian Collector* (May / June, 1980), pp. 39-43.

Ryder, Huia G. *Antique Furniture by New Brunswick Craftsmen.* Toronto: Ryerson, 1965.

Saint Pierre, Angeline. *Médard Bourgault, Sculpteur.* Québec: Éditions Garneau, 1973.

———. *L'oeuvre de Médard Bourgault.* Québec: Éditions Garneau, 1976.

Saskatchewan Primitives. Saskatoon: Mendel Art Gallery, 1975.

Saskatoon Early Images. Saskatoon: Saskatoon Heritage Society, 1982.

Scenes of Charlevoix. Montréal: Montréal Museum of Fine Arts, 1981.

Sculpture traditionnel du Québec. Québec Musée du Québec, 1967.

Séguin, Robert-Lionel. *Les moules du Québec.* Ottawa: National Museum of Canada, 1963.

Seven Saskatchewan Folk Artists. Regina: Norman Mackenzie Art Gallery, 1976.

Shackleton, Philip. *The Furniture of Old Ontario*. Toronto: Macmillan of Canada, 1973.

Shadbolt, Doris. 'Our Relation to Primitive Art.' *Canadian Art* (October / November, 1947), pp. 14-16.

Sotheby's, Toronto. Auction Catalogues (May 5-6, 1981; October 6-7, 1981).

Stevenson, Sheila. *Colchester Furniture Makers*. Truro, Nova Scotia: Colchester Historical Museum, 1979.

Tarasoff, Koozma J. *A Pictorial History of the Doukhobors*. Saskatoon: The Western Producer, 1969.

————. *Traditional Doukhobor Folkways*. Ottawa: National Museum of Man Mercury Series, 1978.

Thériault, Léon. *Images de l'Acadie*. Montréal: Hurtibise, 1980.

Thomas, Jane. 'Folk Art.' *Artswest* (March, 1983), pp. 16-19.

Tilney, Philip V.R. *Artifacts from the CCFCS Collections: Sampling No. 1*. Ottawa: National Museum of Man Mercury Series, 1973.

Toronto Primitives. Toronto: Market Gallery, 1984.

Traquair, Ramsay. 'Hooked Rugs in Canada.' *Canadian Geographical Journal* (May, 1943), pp. 240-254.

Trask, Deborah. *Life How Short, Eternity How Long: Gravestone Carvings and Carvers in Nova Scotia*. Halifax: Nova Scotia Museum, 1978.

'*Twas Ever Thus: A Selection of Eastern Canadian Folk Art*. Toronto: M.F. Feheley, 1979 (Essays by Louis C. Jones, J. Russell Harper, Ralph and Patricia Price).

Trudel, Jean. *La sculpture ancienne du Québec, manifestation d'art populaire*. Montréal: Vie des arts, 1973.

Waddington's Auction Catalogues (June 15-17, 1980; October 6-7, 1981; November 9-11, 1981; June 21-22, 1982; April 2, 1984).

Waller, Adrian. 'Maud Lewis' Fairy-Tale World.' *Reader's Digest* (November, 1983), pp. 122-127.

Watercolour Painting in Saskatchewan 1905-1980. Saskatoon: Mendel Art Gallery, 1980.

Watson, Julie. 'Maud Lewis, Primitive Painter.' *The Atlantic Advocate* (December, 1981), pp. 50-51.

Webster, Donald B. (editor). *The Book of Canadian Antiques*. Toronto: McGraw-Hill Ryerson, 1974.

————. *The William Eby Pottery, Conestogo, Ontario, 1855-1907*. Toronto: Royal Ontario Museum (Occasional Paper No. 25), 1971.

————. *Decorated Stoneware Pottery of North America*. Rutland, Vermont: Tuttle, 1971.

————. *The Brantford Pottery, 1849-1907*. Toronto: Royal Ontario Museum (Occasional Paper No. 13), 1968.

————. *Early Canadian Pottery*. Toronto: McClelland and Stewart, 1971.

Whitehead, Ruth Holmes. *Elitekey: Micmac Material Culture from 1600 AD to the Present*. Halifax: Nova Scotia Museum, 1980.

William Nathaniel Bird Everton: Carvings. Drawings by Harold Barling Town. Toronto: Mazelow Gallery, n.d.

'Wood Carver of Madawaska Has Talent.' Fredericton: *Daily Mail* (April 15, 1937) (on Albert Nadeau).

Widely respected authorities on Canadian folk art, Terry Kobayashi and Michael Bird have made a habit of travelling extensively throughout Canada to engage in first-hand research at museums, archives and in the countryside. Their growing list of folk art publications already includes four books: *Ontario Fraktur: A Pennsylvania German Folk Tradition in Early Canada* (M.F. Feheley: 1977), *A Splendid Harvest: Germanic Folk and Decorative Arts in Canada* (Van Nostrand Reinhold: 1981), *Canadian Folk Art: Old Ways in a New Land* (Oxford University Press: 1983), and *Folk Treasures of Historic Ontario* (with Elizabeth Price, Ontario Heritage Foundation: 1985). Their many articles have appeared in both Canadian and American journals, and they have lectured extensively throughout Canada and the United States. In recent years they have organized some twenty folk art exhibitions which have travelled to museums and galleries in Canada, the United States and Europe. Their personal folk art collection, recently declared a National Treasure, has been acquired by the Joseph Schneider House Museum, where it is made available for scholarly research and public enjoyment. Other items are now with the National Museum of Man (Canadian Centre for Folk Culture Studies) in Ottawa.

Michael teaches in the Religious Studies Department at the University of Waterloo, specializing in religion and the arts. Terry is an Honours Graduate in Art History from the University of Toronto and she teaches art and is department head at Eastwood Collegiate Institute in Kitchener. Their spare time interests include travel abroad, theatre, photography, music (Terry sings in the K-W Philharmonic Choir, and Michael is a jazz pianist), as well as reading, art and culinary enjoyment!

Acknowledgements

Perhaps there should be a companion volume to express proper appreciation to the many persons whose generous contributions have made possible the appearance of the present work. To simply collect the wealth of correspondence with so many kind representatives of galleries, museums, archives, libraries, or relatives of artists would require a volume of several hundred pages in itself. The authors would like, in particular, to single out for special attention the wonderful hospitality and enthusiastic contributions from the following: Dr. Robert Bishop, Alma Houston, Chris Huntington, Reneé Landry, Wesley C. Mattie, Joan Murray, Prof. Nancy-Lou Patterson, Ralph and Patricia Price, Michael Rowan, Dr. Max Stern, George Swinton, David Thauberger and Pastor Frederick S. Weiser.

Our most sincere gratitude goes also to Lynne Bell, Peter and Margaret Bell, Don and Joyce Blythe, Mr. and Mrs. Fred Blayney, Laurie Brinklow, Catherine Bryan, Joan Bulger, Susan Burke, William and Caroline Byfield, Ron and Wendy Cascaden, Catherine Christie, Barbara Coffman, Russell Cooper, Jowe and Pauline Creighton, Mark Cummings, Rev. Ross and the late Alice Cummings, the late Yosef Drenters, Michele Dupuis, Magnus Einarsson, Valerie Evans, Richard and Deborah Henning Field, John and Vikki Forbes, Léopold Foulem, Hyla Fox, Ted Fraser, Terry Graff, Patricia Grattan, Dr. Norman Green, Cora Greenaway, Dr. John and Anne Hall, Frank Halpern, John and Heather Harbison, Heather Hatch, Rick and Holly Henemader, Charles C. Hill, Tom Hill, Don and Myrtle Hoffman, William and Pauline Hogan, Janet Holmes, John Houston, Howard and Pat Jasper, Dr. Louis C. and Agnes Halsey Jones, Pamela Krueger, Thérèse La Tour, Marjorie and Clarence Larmon, Patrick Laurette, Mr. and Mrs. William Leask, Emile Lessard, Bruce Malcolm, Louise McNamara, Petter Millard, Ian Montagnes, the late Hertha Muysson, William Muysson, Judith Nasby, Rev. Larry Neff, Andrew Oko, Cécile Oullet, Sandra Overstrum, Howard Pain, Prof. E. Palmer Patterson, William and Jeanne Pattison, Henry Pauls, Carol Phillips, Mr. and Mrs. Derek Phillips, Elizabeth Price, Bernard Riordan, Lloyd Ryder, John and Miriam Rock, Madeleine Savard, C.N.D., Mrs. Nettie Sharpe, Jim and Marie Sherman, Vernon and Maggie Smart, Barbara Snyder, Alan and Lorna-Lee Snowie, Robert and Brenda Starr, Sam Steiner, Deborah Trask, Edward Theobald, Liza Whealy, Susan Whitney, William Yeager, and others who have extended to us their immeasurable generosity.